The Gifted Puppy Program

LAURIE LEACH

The Gifted Puppy Program

TFH Publications®
President/CEO: Glen S. Axelrod
Executive Vice President: Mark E. Johnson
Publisher: Albert Connelly, Jr.
Associate Publisher: Stephanie Fornino

Project Team
Editors: Stephanie Fornino,
    Matthew Haviland
Indexer: Dianne L. Schneider
Designer: Angela Stanford

TFH Publications, Inc.®
One TFH Plaza
Third and Union Avenues
Neptune City, NJ 07753

Printed and bound in China
15 16 17 18 19 20   1 3 5 7 9 8 6 4 2

Library of Congress Cataloging-in-Publication Data
Leach, Laurie.
  The gifted puppy program : 40 games, activities, and exercises to raise a brilliant, happy dog / Laurie Leach.
    pages cm
  Includes bibliographical references and index.
  ISBN 978-0-7938-0721-5 (pbk. : alk. paper)
1. Puppies--Training. 2. Puppies--Behavior. 3. Dogs--Training. I. Title.
SF431.L386 2015
636.7'07--dc23
          2014039195

The Leader In Responsible Animal Care For Over 50 Years!®
www.tfh.com

Table of Contents

Introduction

Whether you have a puppy or adult dog, it's never too late to stretch his mind.

This is not just another book about housetraining pups. This how-to book is about raising a canine partner who is primed for anything you might want to do, from organized sports to playing games in the backyard. It is built on a simple premise that the more a puppy learns, the more he is capable of learning. By investing just a bit more time teaching your pup, you can raise a canine pal who knows dozens of games and commands and whose capacity for learning has increased exponentially.

Who Can Use This Book?

You may be interested in this book because you are looking for guidance in raising your first pup. You have come to the right place. The majority of my students are new or relatively new to owning a puppy. They have tested and successfully used all of the exercises in the book with their own pups of every size and breed.

On the other hand, you may have bought this book because you are an experienced trainer or dog sport competitor looking for more games to play with your new pup. You already understand that it is ideal to super-charge your puppy raising. Even if you fall into these groups, I feel confident that you will find activities in this book that you have not taught before.

But what if you have an older pup or adult dog? It is important to note that this training program is equally valuable for these dogs. It is never too late to stretch your dog's mind. A number of folks joined our Gifted Puppy Program, a training group dedicated to stretching our dogs' minds, with adult dogs. Who could say no? What we found was that the dogs enjoyed the training challenges and clearly grew in confidence and willingness to work.

How This Book Is Organized
This book falls into two categories:

Section 1
The first six chapters provide background that teaches you to think like a dog, reveals professional dog trainers' key secrets, and addresses practical matters such as picking the right training equipment and using a clicker.

Section 2
In the second section, you will launch into 40 activities broken down by the following five behavioral focus areas:
1. Relationship building

When dogs are presented with training challenges, their confidence grows, as does their willingness to learn.

If you take the time to train your pup, you'll enrich both his life and yours.

2. Everyday behaviors
3. Socialization and confidence building
4. Attention and self-control
5. Just for fun

Each exercise lists the following information:
- goal of the exercise
- ideal age to start
- groundwork needed to learn the exercise
- whether a clicker is required
- background information on what you should know prior to beginning the training
- step-by-step instructions on how to train the exercise
- possible challenges

It is my hope that this book will be tattered and dirty by the time your pup is grown. I hope that you will write in the margins about what worked and what you learned.

Bonus Information

In addition to encouraging you to teach your dog a wide variety of games and commands, I hope to deepen your understanding of dog training in general in a painless way. Within each activity, you will find two bonus sidebars:

- **Real-Life Pups:** I have included a section titled "Real-Life Pups" that showcases a pup who actually learned the command or how to play the game. There is nothing better than "seeing" another pup doing something cool to brush away doubts about what you and your pup (or dog) can accomplish.

- **Trainer Talk:** Second, I have included a short section within each activity called "Trainer Talk" that highlights key points and important concepts about dog training in general.

The pups who are highlighted belong to students and friends. One friend shared a number of her experiences with teaching her Border Collie pup, Jade. I have also included tales and photos of many pups being raised as future assistance dogs. On occasion, I have included a story about my dogs, current and past. They represent a full range of dogs, from my sled dog of years ago to my current Shelties, Papillon, and Border Collies. Besides, they are always on my mind since they like scattering around me as I write and letting me know when we need to take a break for a game.

The Road to Enrichment

You may never have thought that you needed more than a typical pet dog who goes on walks and likes to take rides in the car. You may have imagined taking your pup though one obedience class and calling it a day with training. The odds are good that if you are still reading this book, you are someone who wants the best possible life for your pup—and dog. I promise that if you leap in and tap all the intelligence and willingness to work that your dog has to offer, you will enrich both his life and yours.

Part 1
Not All Puppyhoods
Are Created Equal

There is a puppy in my house as I write this. It highlights for me, once again, the choice we encounter when we raise a young canine. We can housetrain them, teach them to walk on a leash, and show them how to sit and lie down. We can leave it at that. Or we can take the next step and recognize that our pups (and dogs) are capable of so much more.

In this first section, I am going to do my best to talk you into this second point of view. I will start with the first chapter by making a case for teaching your canine pal the same way we teach gifted children: by providing extensive enrichment and opportunities to learn.

In the second chapter, we will look at canine intelligence and whether dogs are up to the training challenge. We will talk about their rich emotional life and their highly developed social skills. We will discuss the impact of these factors on your puppy raising.

However, there is a bit of danger in recognizing how capable puppies and dogs are. In the third chapter, we will discuss the unfortunate trend of treating dogs as if they are our children. We will consider the specific ways in which dogs are different from humans and why they deserve to be trained using strategies that match their view of the world.

We can teach our pups in the same way that we teach gifted children: by providing them with extensive enrichment and opportunities to learn.

The proper training equipment will provide you with powerful tools to communicate with your dog.

In the fourth chapter, we'll review training methods that make sense to dogs. You'll also learn the top ten secrets that top professional dog trainers know. (They are not mysterious.) Although it is good to internalize these guidelines, you don't need to commit them to memory all at once. You will find them embedded throughout the activities in the book, so you can learn them over time as you work with your pup.

We will wrap up this section with a discussion of clicker training and training equipment selection. Both the clicker and use of the correct training equipment will provide you with powerful, positive tools to communicate with your dog.

My pup just let me know that she is up now. With clicker in hand and a pocketful of treats, we are off to the yard to reinforce her housetraining and to begin a new game.

Chapter 1
A Good Puppy Mind Is a Terrible Thing to Waste

I came to understand that any puppy raiser who invested the energy could raise a gifted puppy in an unusual way. For many years, I led mostly parallel lives—public school educator by day, dog trainer by night and weekend. In the first capacity, I taught English to high school students, striving enthusiastically to eliminate the run-on sentence. When I left school each day, I trained my own sled dogs, obedience dogs, and agility dogs. I helped others to work with their pet dogs, performance dogs, and assistance dogs in training. Other than those rare occasions when my ninth graders said, with good humor, "You're using the dog voice on us again," there were few overlaps in my two worlds.

In my capacity as an educator, I was passionate about helping students to learn greater breadth and depth of material. One pilot program caught my eye. In this program, "regular" youngsters were challenged with schoolwork often

All puppy raisers are capable of raising gifted pups.

reserved for those children who were labeled as "gifted." The result was stunning. It quickly became very difficult to tell which students were labeled as gifted through testing and which youngsters had blossomed because of the opportunities they were given. The bottom line is that if you assume that a healthy child is gifted and set out to teach her as such, she will stretch beyond anyone's wildest imagination.

My two worlds collided. I began to wonder what this epiphany about teaching children meant for puppy raising. What would happen if all pups were treated as if they were gifted? What if we assumed that our pups are capable of learning much more than we had ever thought possible? What if we created the equivalent of gifted education for our canine pals?

Designing a Gifted Program for Puppies

I always have a small pack of dogs of different ages at home. My pups and my training classes became my first experiment as I set out to design a program for stimulating and stretching puppy minds in the same way we were challenging students at school.

My goal was to create a puppy curriculum that would encourage my pups and those in puppy classes to do the following:

- work eagerly and happily with their handler
- display confidence in a wide variety of settings
- learn traditional basic commands
- master dozens of additional commands and activities
- perform complex tasks, which involve responding to a series of commands

After deciding on these outcomes, I scoured many sources to select activities and games that would keep pups learning and thinking. My students and I began to incorporate new types of exercises that went much beyond the traditional obedience exercises such as *sit* and *down* and *stay*. We began to teach the pups games such as how to spin right and left, how to search for hidden cookies, and how to play hide-and-seek. We began to teach them new commands such as *hurry*, *spin*, and *high five*. We expanded our socialization much earlier in the pups' lives to include outings to the ATM and small shopping centers. We regarded pups as learning sponges, ready and willing to absorb skills and learning behaviors as long as we presented them at the correct level and in a positive context. All in all, we did our best to create a gifted program for our pups.

My thoughts about a new way of raising pups didn't develop in isolation. About the same time that I was beginning to think about teaching pups in a new way, kindergarten puppy classes appeared on the dog training scene. It seemed that every dog training club added a kindergarten class to their list

The Gifted Puppy Program is about enriching your dog's life with a variety of games and activities.

of offerings. This was a brilliant concept for introducing pups to new experiences, surfaces, and sounds. These classes seemed to me to be an essential component of any program for raising a gifted pup. However, the classes didn't go nearly far enough in my mind. The Gifted Puppy Program is about teaching your pup for at least a year and forever enriching his life with a variety of activities.

The Results

The results were clear very quickly. All of the pups who were asked to learn more, using positive methods, responded just as the children had who were treated as if they were gifted. The more we taught them, the more they were capable and eager to learn. At the end of a year, the handlers who stuck with the program had taught their pups as many as 50 commands and games. Every puppy had learned to do things that made traditional puppy training, which teaches five or six commands, look like the Dark Ages. Even more importantly, the pups had grown into dogs who were extraordinarily eager to learn, work, and play with their human partners.

A New Dimension

After a few years of piloting the Gifted Puppy Program in public classes, I was hired to teach the puppy training classes for Canine Companions for Independence (CCI). CCI is

The more commands your pup knows, the better you'll appreciate him as a member of the family.

the original school that raises and trains dogs to assist people with different disabilities.

Puppy raisers receive their pups at 8 weeks and train them until 16 months, when the pups are returned to CCI for advanced training. The pups are expected to master 30 commands, and puppy raisers are also expected to socialize these Labrador/Golden Retriever crosses to everything they might encounter later as a service dog working with a disabled person, a facility dog working at a school or hospital, or a hearing dog working with a hearing-impaired partner.

These classes provided an interesting new lab because I had never taught many of the commands that CCI gave me. For example, pups had to learn to heel on both the right and left sides of their handler. In addition, they had to learn more complex behaviors such as crawling under a table and lying quietly and resting quietly in the puppy raiser's lap while getting dressed in a CCI cape and Gentle Leader headcollar. Many of the commands were attractive to me because they were so useful. Every one made the pup a greater joy to have around the house.

Puppies who learn through kind, age-appropriate training are happier pets.

I gradually learned the best ways to help the puppy raisers, an interesting mix of folks who had never owned a dog and people who had raised a dozen pups for a CCI. Although these pups are generally sweet, compliant animals, there was still a wide range of activity levels and willingness to work that put our teaching methods to the test.

After teaching classes for generations of CCI pups, I am more convinced than ever that we have underestimated puppies for eons. It is not even a stretch to teach a pup 30 commands by the time he is a year old.

As a result of this program, I gradually revised the commands and exercises that I taught in my public classes. I substituted the practical commands from CCI for the less important tricks that we had taught early on. For example, it is lovely having a pup who will lie quietly across your lap for brushing.

Do I Need a Gifted Puppy?

You might wonder why you need a gifted pup. As I mentioned in the Introduction, you may have never thought you needed more than a typical pet dog. But if you are reading this book, the odds are good that you are someone who wants the most fulfilling life possible for your pup. Here is why the Gifted Puppy Program promises the best for your new pal:

- Puppies who learn more, through kind, age-appropriate training, are simply happier. Dogs actively enjoy learning. A friend of mine often says, "A good dog mind is a terrible thing to waste." If you stop teaching your pup at six months, it is like pulling a child out of school in the second grade.

- Puppies love to get out and about. They are inquisitive creatures. This program will provide a framework for you to provide your pup with experiences that include a wide range of new people, sights, and sounds. This builds a relaxed confidence that will serve your dog his whole life.
- Pups thrive when they have a few minutes of your undivided time several times a day.
- Teaching your pup deepens your relationship in a way that just hanging out cannot do. Working and playing together builds trust and respect between you and your pup.
- This program lays a foundation for any activities you might want to do with your dog, from informal activities such as hiking together to organized games such as agility or rally.

You may wonder if you have time to teach your puppy so many things. There is no need to quit your day job, but it is important to make two commitments. First, if you can set aside 20 minutes a day (divided into shorter sessions of five to ten minutes) for "formal" lessons and playing, you are on the right track. Secondly, if you can fully integrate your pup into your daily life, you will observe that he is learning all the time. In a few minutes of teaching, you can take advantage of those experiences. For example, a walk to the mailbox can be a great time to practice the casual *heel* or appropriate ways to meet and greet new people. If you don't have any specific time to dedicate to a young animal, you might want to hold off getting a pup.

Components of the Gifted Puppy Program

After several years of implementing this program with multiple generations of puppies, I have developed tried and true exercises that provide pups with a wide range of opportunities to learn. These include traditional commands and exposure to a variety of novel and stimulating experiences. These activities have sorted themselves into five categories:
1. Relationship Building
2. Everyday Behaviors
3. Socialization & Confidence Building
4. Attention & Self-Control
5. Just for Fun

In the following sections of this book, you will find multiple games to teach your pup in each of these categories. Each lesson identifies its primary focus.

Just the Right Word

In writing any book, the author makes daily decisions to use this word or that. In this book, I struggled a bit with using the words that best captured what I meant. Let me share my thoughts briefly.

Traditionally, those of us who live with dogs have called ourselves "owners." In this book I will continue to use that word although I think it is flawed. I do not feel that I own my dogs. They definitely have minds of their own and they show that regularly when we play and train. Other folks clearly feel the same way about the term, and in recent years, there has been a trend to use the word "guardian." This word sounds much too passive to me. I do much more than guard my dogs. Our lives together are intensely interactive. I ask them to work with me and treat them as my friends. I mention this in the hope that you might help me come up with the perfect term.

Another conscious choice I made was whether to use the terms "train" and "trainer" when referring to the process of teaching a pup. In reality, I think of myself as teaching my pups and of myself as their teacher. It is a subtle but important difference. I think of training as getting my dog to do some behavior using an understandable series of steps. I think of teaching as getting my dog to *want* to do some behavior and to enjoy both the learning and final result. In the end, I have decided to use the two words interchangeably, but I will remind you periodically that the process should be sequential and joyful to you and your pup.

In the same vein, I have struggled with the word "command," a word traditionally used to tell the dog what we want him to do. *Sit* and *speak* are commands. The word exudes a sense that we are in a high position and have the power to control a situation. The reality is that we can command all we want, but unless our pups decide to cooperate for a variety of reasons, we won't

The goal of teaching your dog is to convince him to want to perform a behavior and simultaneously enjoy the process.

get the results we want. My search for an alternative went nowhere, so I have used this word. When you see it, consider it to mean that you are attaching a sound to some behavior or task we want our pup to do.

Lastly, I have thought about the best words to describe the behaviors included in the book, some designed to raise a good canine citizen and others intended to stimulate your pup's mental capacity. I have used the words "exercises," "activities," and "games" for variety. Although "exercise" sounds more serious than "game," there is no difference intended. All of them should be fun for your pup and have value in his development as a gifted pup.

Different Breeds, Different Challenges

Dogs come in a stunning array of sizes and energy levels. Some are serious couch potatoes. Others can bring a flock of sheep a hundred miles over rough terrain with minimal help from humans. Some dogs are inherently devoted. I cannot go from room to room without my current Shelties getting up to follow me. Other breeds give cats a run for their money in terms of independence.

Not all pups arrive with the same enthusiasm for learning. For example, I once raced a team of northern breeds. Although these pups and dogs happily learned dozens of games and commands, I never trusted them to come to me in an open area. The genetic programming of a sled dog to run toward that far horizon is simply too strong. One must

Different breeds come with different traits; the Australian Shepherd, for example, is known for his boundless energy.

be a realist. On the other hand, their lives were much richer as a result of the extensive training we did together. They actively enjoyed weaving through my legs or spinning right and left—as long as the gate was locked.

No matter what background your pup brings to your partnership, an ongoing puppy training program will improve his mind and increase his willingness to work with you. Just recognize that the more independent breeds will require more repetitions and more reinforcement. In the end, every puppy (and dog) can learn a huge amount if you approach the process in a spirit of fun and keep your sense of humor.

If you haven't yet selected your pup, it is important to make sure that the animal with whom you will share your life is a good match. I recently worked with a lovely, quiet woman who had impulsively purchased an Australian Shepherd, a high-energy breed. Her life has become a whirlwind of training classes and dog parks, but she still feels guilty that her dog is not getting adequate exercise.

Finding the right breed or mix of breeds requires adequate research. If you are a quiet person, find a quiet breed with a history as a companion dog. If you have a prize garden, consider breeds that are not especially programmed to dig. If you want a pal to keep up with your busy schedule every day, then a herding or working breed may be just the right match.

Your pup comes with an amazing capacity to learn the ways of the world with you as his teacher.

In Conclusion

In her book *For the Love of a Dog*, Patricia McConnell says it so well when she writes, "Many studies show the importance of an enriched environment. Ironically the general public, responsible for the lives of over sixty million dogs a year in just the United States alone, is often less aware of enrichment's importance. My associates and I often see dogs raised in conditions designed to handicap the development of their minds, not encourage it."

This book is about encouraging the development of your pup's mind. It is about teaching and stimulating your pup until he is at least a young adult. I hope that once you try the Gifted Puppy Program, you will find it impossible to conceive of teaching a puppy less.

As we get started, shake off old assumptions that you might have about what your pup can learn. He comes with an amazing capacity to learn the ways of the world with you as his teacher. Don't let that good puppy mind go to waste.

Chapter 2
Smarter Than You Think

This chapter and the next are attached at the hip. In this chapter, I will encourage you to recognize that your pup is smarter and more emotional than you might expect. This is an essential concept if your goal is to maximize that intelligence and raise a gifted pup. In the next chapter, we will switch gears and consider the ways in which our pups are different from us. I will encourage you to recognize that dogs, in spite of their multiple intelligences, are relatively innocent creatures who do not think like us or perceive the world in the way we do. This awareness allows us to teach our pups using strategies that they understand, and it keeps us from expecting things they can't deliver, such as recognizing the difference between chewing on a stick and chewing on the siding of the house. In the end, it is my goal to convince you that your puppy is brilliant, but his brilliance and way of learning are different than yours.

Pups who live in enriched environments have a higher capacity for understanding and performing new tasks.

There are dozens of books about how dogs think and feel and act, written by a variety of authors who have studied many dogs. This chapter is just the tip of the iceberg. If you find a canine's inner world fascinating, there are many resources to explore.

Research about canine learning is ongoing. I was fascinated by a study in which dogs learned how to earn a treat by watching other dogs and mimicking their behavior, even if they had never seen the behavior before. In this case, the behavior was using their mouth rather than paw to trigger a treat-releasing device. If you are an avid observer of dogs, you may greet such studies with an eye roll and a nod, but it is good to have science back up what we already know.

While information about the puppy brain is interesting, this is a book about teaching your pup. To make that link, each of the topics below will include a few comments on the implications for training.

A Brain in Waiting

Just like people, pups have more brain than they often use. The rest of that brain is just sitting there waiting for the call to action.

Most dogs live lives in which they tap just enough of their brain cells to get by. Lucky pups who live in an enriched environment with places to go and things to do build more neural pathways, the tiny freeways of the brain, to new parts of the brain. With each new "road" in the brain, a pup's capacity for understanding and performing new tasks expands.

Recently, human physiologists announced that neural pathways can continue to be built in every healthy brain regardless of age. The key is stimulation. It makes sense that this is also true for canines. I notice no difference between teaching a new skill to my pup or to my ten-year-old Papillon.

Implications for Puppy Raising

This information directly matches what I observed in school classrooms. The bottom line is that much of that puppy brain will go to waste if you don't put it to work.

Will Work for Pay

Both dogs and humans share yet another important characteristic: We repeat behaviors for which we are positively reinforced. For example, when humans go to work, they get paid. As a result, they go back. In the same way, pups repeat behaviors for which they get reinforced. A dog who gets rewarded several times after he sits will want to sit again.

Dogs repeat behaviors for which they are positively reinforced.

Your puppy knows whether or not sniffing in the yard provides a bigger "paycheck" than coming when you call.

There are four specific ways to "pay" your pup: food, toys, play, and interactions with you. In Chapter 4, we'll discuss the specifics of when and where you should deliver those during training. For most pups, but certainly not all, the favored reinforcement is food. My older Sheltie Scout will do a one-leg handstand for food, but petting annoys her. My young Sheltie Boo values petting and verbal praise far above anything else I can provide. And Cyder the Labrador will try anything if she knows I will reward her by tossing the tennis ball. One of your first challenges is to discover what your pup perceives as rewarding so that you can use it while you are teaching him the ways of the world.

Implications for Puppy Raising

Understanding that you have to pay your pup for his hard work is at the heart of all effective puppy training. That is, if a pup doesn't do something you want (assuming he understands your directions), you have simply not made it worth his while.

Puppy raisers often tell me that their pup no longer comes when called. If your pup doesn't come to you, he is saying that the environment is paying off more than you are. If you want him to come, the pay has to be worthwhile from his point of view. All puppies will do what pays best.

This concept rubs many folks the wrong way. They simply want their pup to *want* to come. Remember our basic premise that dogs are smarter than we think? Your pup knows whether or not sniffing in the yard provides a bigger paycheck than coming into the house at your bidding. The heart of all puppy training is to figure out how to convince your pup that working with you is better than his enjoyment elsewhere. Pups and dogs are brilliant at understanding which behavior is in their best interest.

Food Treats: Bribery or Something More?

There is no shortage of theories about training dogs and pups. Trainers often joke that there are as many methods as there are trainers. Most folks recognize that there are dozens of effective ways to teach a pup any particular command or activity. However, there is one topic that generates heated discussion among trainers.

This issue focuses on the use of food while teaching a pup. Some folks maintain that it is bribery to use food in training and creates dependence on food. Folks in this camp believe that you shouldn't have to pay your pup with food to work with you.

I stand firmly in the opposite camp. I think that this belief is silly. We value money. Dogs value food. I know I wouldn't continue to do much of what I do if I never got paid. Stanley Coren, author of *How Dogs Think*, reminds us that dogs originally teamed up with people who lived in caves in exchange for scraps: "It might not be far-fetched to say that the contract we humans have with dogs to obtain their loyalty and assistance is signed in food. By giving our dogs food treats for their obedience and their service, we simply honor that ancient contract." I strongly support the wise use of food to teach your dog, and I will show you how.

Use food tidbits to teach, encourage, and reinforce your dog.

Implications for Puppy Raising

In the activities you will be doing with your pup, I will encourage you to use tidbits of food to teach, encourage, and reinforce him in many ways. You will reduce the use of food over time as your pup understands each game, but it should never go away entirely. If you took Psychology 101, you may remember the concept of "extinction." It said that if a behavior is never reinforced, it goes away. Poof.

Naturally, toy play, petting, and praise are good ways to reward your dog too. But don't toss out the dog cookie jar.

Socially Gifted Animals

Like humans, dogs are immensely social. In fact, social hierarchy is their lens for organizing the world. They constantly know where they fit in relation to other dogs with whom they live or play, and they know where they fit in relation to their owners.

This intelligence is highly developed. For example, when new pups gather in a class, they quickly sort themselves by rank, often with communication of which we are unaware. However, if a new pup joins the class, there is an immediate awareness of the newcomer and an interest in figuring out where he fits. In a multi-dog household, there is an established hierarchy. When a new pup arrives, the order of things re-establishes itself.

The reality is that dogs do flourish with clear, consistent leadership from their humans. Given their natural understanding of social order, they flourish under a kindly leader who clearly communicates and enforces the rules. My three dogs follow me around the house all day like an extended shadow. No way can I leave the room without them getting up, which often makes me feel bad when I get up for the 45th time. Each of them knows how things are done here. As soon as we get out of bed, they go outside and do toilettes. During the day, they can get on the furniture when invited and they get off or move when asked to. When meals are served, they lie down and wait to be invited to their bowl. No dog bothers another dog who is still eating. At bedtime, they go into their crates next to the bed to sleep. None of this is open for negotiation. There know there are times we play together and times that individual dogs get to work with me. The result of having clear rules is that dogs live stress-free because they do not need to

Dogs flourish when they receive clear, consistent leadership from their humans.

worry about the unexpected.

There is a current fad in dog training based on a dog's social nature. The premise is that you need to assert yourself as the pack leader with dogs. There is certainly some truth to this. Dogs will take charge of a household if allowed to. Unfortunately, the mindset of pack leadership can lead to dangerous conclusions. The idea of being in charge has sometimes been construed to mean dominance. This easily translates to punishing rather than teaching dogs and can take the form of hitting, berating, or isolating them. These interactions never lead to better behavior. Punishing does create pups who are scared, sneaky, and sometimes aggressive because they feel they must protect themselves.

Implications for Puppy Raising

There are three important implications for raising your pup. First, when you bring your pup home, it is important to establish yourself as his leader. He will be happiest if he understands that you are in charge and that he is safe. In her book *Parenting Your Dog*,

Use a training tool such as a crate to teach your pup that spending time alone is okay for a bit.

behaviorist Trish King describes this role as identical to good child parenting. You must have high standards for your pup and provide lots of support to help him meet them. If your standard is that your pup won't piddle in the house, then you need to set up a positive system in which he never has a chance to make that mistake. Just like a good parent, successful puppy raisers never try to overpower or scare a pup into behaving.

The second implication is that your role as pack leader brings responsibilities. In the wild, canines were taught by the adults in the pack. In our homes, it is our job to teach our pups to live well in our environment using clear, positive strategies. This book includes detailed instructions you can follow to teach your pup from the day he comes home until he is an adult. Sadly, many puppy raisers simply hope that their pup will learn how to behave on his own, which inevitably has disastrous results.

The third implication may not be as obvious. As socially gifted animals, pups do not take well to being left alone. In fact, time alone often makes them very anxious. With most pups, it takes specific training and use of training tools such as the crate to teach a pup that he is okay on his own for a bit. Pups who don't learn this lesson are often amazingly destructive. I often think of my normally gentle neighbor shrieking after his terrier pup had eaten the irrigation pipe in his backyard for the fourth time.

When training your dog, keep him relaxed and joyful—you want him in the best state of mind for learning.

A Rich Emotional Life

There has been an avalanche of interest in recent years about how pups think and what they feel. For decades, this never crossed my mind. Now I wonder almost daily what is going on inside those furry heads.

Scientists maintain that the question of whether pups and dogs have emotions can't be tested. I can only say, get a dog. It is impossible to live with a pup longer than five minutes and not know that he feels a variety of emotions. It is not clear if those emotions are exactly the same as we feel, but there is no doubt in my mind that pups and dogs experience a wide range of feelings.

I believe that dogs and pups feel, at the least, joy, anxiety/fear, loneliness, contentment, excitement, disappointment, and impatience. How do I know? I see the joy when Scout gets her special time on the bed in the morning. She moans happily in a way that she never does at another time in the day. I observed Boo's fear of loud noises when he was a pup. I see Cyder's disappointment any time I tell her that she can't go in the car with me. On the other hand, you can't imagine a happier dog when I invite her along.

Implications for Puppy Raising

Emotions have everything to do with learning for people and pups. In the classroom, I knew ninth graders could learn the most if they were happy and relaxed. If I had a bad day and made them anxious or resentful in some way, their learning took a dive. Puppies are exactly the same. If you teach your pup so that he enjoys each lesson as a game, he will learn faster than you can imagine.

The other night I observed an interesting situation. One of the puppies in class looked visibly resentful; there was just something in his body language and expression. When his handler asked him to follow commands he did it, but clearly under protest. Later when I talked with the handler, I found that she had not trained the pup for two weeks. On class day, she trained him a lot. By the time he got to class, he was already tired, overworked, and definitely not having a good time. This pressure hurts rather than helps a pup to learn.

When you are teaching your little partner, keep him relaxed and joyful. If you watch his eyes, mouth, ears, and posture, you will learn to read how he is feeling and adjust what you are doing to keep him in the best state of mind for learning. When in doubt, smile a lot and laugh frequently. Pups are very capable of recognizing your expressions and sounds of joy.

In Conclusion

Your little pup has it all: brains, a wide range of emotions, and highly developed social intelligence. Once you recognize what a capable partner he is and what a powerful interest he has in working with you, you have taken the first step toward raising a gifted pup. Now let's take a look at how your canine pal actually learns.

Chapter 3
Not Little People in Fur Coats

Dogs think very differently than humans do, and they deserve to be treated in ways that make sense to them.

A few years ago, it was common to hear that a growing number of dog lovers had started treating their pup as a member of the family. I was excited about this. It meant that more dogs were living in the house rather than isolated in the backyard. I imagined more folks leaving on vacation with their canine pal in the back of the car instead of a kennel. In fact, in a survey conducted by a national veterinary organization, a whopping 67 percent of dog owners said they had taken their pet on vacation. These changes seemed to be a good thing, recognition of our intense and complex relationship with our dogs.

But the changes did not stop there. A significant group of dog owners began humanizing their dogs, treating them not just as a family member but as a child. However, there are many problems with trying to turn dogs into people. When we think of our pup as a mini-me, we make assumptions and act in ways that confuse him or set him up to make mistakes. Many folks who arrive at a puppy class are clearly overindulging their pups with food and toys. They are afraid to tell their pup no firmly lest they hurt his feelings. In extreme cases, they give in to what the dog wants until he has taken over the house. Treat your pup as something other than a pup and there is a good chance that you will raise a dog with anxiety or even aggression issues.

I am not guilt-free. I have caught myself referring to pups' owners as their "parents." I occasionally put words in my dogs' mouths such as, "I love you so much. I worship the ground…" You get the point. But when the time comes to work together, I know that they are sweet, intelligent animals who perceive the world differently than I do and who think differently than I do, and they deserve to be treated in ways that make sense to them.

In this chapter, we are going to focus on the specific ways in which pups are different from humans. I notice in working with puppy raisers that it is much harder to grasp the differences between our species than the similarities. For example, we want to believe that our pups understand the meaning of our chatter. They don't. We want to believe that they recognize right and wrong. They really don't. The more you can internalize these differences, the more effective you will be as a teacher for your pup.

White Noise

The first significant difference between pups and us is that they do not understand language. Our words flow over them like a river. They can, of course, learn to associate specific words or phrases with a behavior, after adequate repetition. For example, they can learn that "wait" means they should stop and stand still. However, they could learn to stop and stand still just as effectively if you snapped your fingers. Any consistent sound can be used to communicate with dogs.

There was a popular greeting card a few years ago that captured this concept. A guy was talking to his dog. In the text box it said, "Blah, blah, blah, blah, Rover, blah, blah." It is fair to say that pups undoubtedly enjoy the sound of our voice used kindly, but except for key words that acquire meaning, it is simply white noise.

You're probably nodding right now. When I talk about this in puppy class everyone nods knowingly. Then when we introduce a new command, what do you think is the first thing that happens? The handlers start chanting the meaningless word at their pup: "Roll, roll, roll." We love words. We are hardwired to talk. Deep in our hearts we believe that if the pup hears that sound one more time, he will magically compute what he is supposed to do. If you can overcome this tendency, you will actually help your pup learn more quickly.

Puppy raisers often overestimate their pup or dog's ability to understand language. If you have a pup who has already learned some commands, you can play a game to test his genuine understanding of language. Pick a word such as "sit," which you believe your puppy or dog knows. Now lie flat on your back on the floor and ask your dog to sit. Odds are very good that your dog will show no recognition of the command once your body language cues and the context in which

Dogs do not understand language, although they learn to associate words or phrases with behaviors.

you usually ask him to sit are removed.

Dogs do not think in words, as people do. Their thoughts are coded differently. When they think, it is most likely a set of pictures. Right now your pup may be picturing a favorite toy in the hopes that you will play with him. These pictures are probably drawn from his heightened senses of smell and hearing as well as his life experience. Right now, my dogs are picturing me standing up and going out to the backyard to play a quick game of flying disc. I'll be right back.

The most effective trainers minimize the use of language while training their dogs.

Implications for Puppy Raising

The best trainers minimize the use of language in teaching pups. This is because a given word means nothing to the pup initially and just distracts from the behavior the trainer is teaching. In the games that follow, I recommend that you do 30 to 50 repetitions of a new behavior before you say the command word at all. This will give your pup a chance to concentrate on what you are asking without having to worry about a nonsense sound you are making. Then we will perform 30 to 50 repetitions saying the command while the pup actually does the behavior. For example, you will say "sit" or "down" while your pup is in the process of sitting or lying down. This will help him pair the sound with the action and guarantees 100 percent success in doing it correctly. Next, we will perform a similar number of repetitions using the command a bit earlier, just when your pup's body language indicates that he is going to do the behavior. For example, when he's about to sit, you'll see that his rear just starts to drop. Again, your pup will simply hear the sound when he is doing the right thing. There is no pressure for him to figure out why you are saying that meaningless noise. Once he has had lots of chances to practice what you are asking, you will finally use the command word to initiate the behavior.

In the games and exercise that follow, I will occasionally remind you how to use this system. The process may seem lengthy. It is. It is worth the investment because your pup will be able to do what you ask reliably and in a variety of settings. When I ask puppy raisers if their pup knows a certain command, the most common answer is, "Most of the time." This book is about teaching your pup so that he knows his commands well enough that you can answer, "Every time, any place."

A Puppy's Senses

This next difference between dogs and humans serves as a good reminder that our pups are descended from wild canines that survived because of predatory skills. Although they have undergone many generations of selective breeding, puppies and dogs still receive information about the world differently than humans do. We see the world with our eyes and then we hear or smell things. Dogs smell and hear their world first. Then they take a look to see if their nose and ears have given them the right information.

A puppy's nose is a stunningly powerful organ. It can distinguish how many dogs have piddled on the curb in front of your house. It can pick up a molecule from the treat in your pocket. You have probably heard that some dogs have been trained to sniff out skin cancer. It's hard to grasp what it would be like to have a nose thousands of times more effective than ours, but such is your pup's world.

Your pup's ability to hear is not far behind. It is most likely hundreds of times better than ours. This means that everyday noises may sometimes overwhelm or startle dogs. Some dogs, particularly herding breeds, are prone to sound sensitivity, but the world must be a cacophony for every pup.

Dogs' eyes record a world that bears little resemblance to the world we see. Although dogs can see better than humans in low light, their daytime vision is quite grainy and less focused at certain

The training process may seem lengthy, but it's worth it because your pup will learn to do what you ask reliably and in a variety of settings.

distances. Have you noticed that your dog sometimes gets startled when you come into the house a different way or wear a strange hat he has never seen? If he does not catch your scent, his vision is simply not clear enough to be sure it is you. In general, it's hard for dogs to see you when you are standing still, but they can always find you when you move a bit. Your dog is an expert at reading your movement. The most recent research suggests that dogs do see colors but not the full palette that human eyes receive. Apparently their world is similar to someone's who is color blind. This is important because your pup may not see a certain toy or object that is obvious to you.

Implications for Puppy Raising

As pups grow up, they encounter dozens of smells, sounds, and sights they are not genetically programmed to understand. In one hour your pup might hear the backfire of a car and the howl of the vacuum cleaner. He might see a stranger in sunglasses and a hat or encounter an elderly person with a cane. Any of these interactions can startle your pup. It is up to us as puppy raisers to actively teach our pups to accept all the things they will encounter in their lives. This is, in fact, the most important aspect of raising a pup.

Interestingly, dog behaviorists agree that the window for teaching a pup the ways of the world slides shut at a very young age. Some scientists put it at 12 weeks and others at about 16 weeks. In my experience, pups who are provided with plenty of experiences between eight weeks and four months learn to take our crazy world in stride. On the other hand, a pup kept isolated too long (beyond 16 weeks) is likely to be fearful and perhaps aggressive when confronted with new experiences. That puts some serious responsibility on you those first two months after your pup arrives home.

What does it mean if you rescue a pup or young dog who has passed the 16-week mark? Give him a day or two to settle in and then embark on all of the socialization exercises described in this book as if he were a baby. While it may take more work, I have seen some pups and dogs

A dog's nose is extremely powerful—thousands of times more effective than a human's nose.

who got off to a bad start prove themselves to be remarkably resilient in adjusting to an expanded world.

The formal term "socialization" refers to the process of introducing pups to the world in which they will live. In the training activities that follow, you will find specific exercises for socializing your pup. These include trips into your neighborhood when your pup is young and lots of field trips before he approaches four months.

Breed-Specific Behaviors

Dog breeds come hardwired for certain behaviors. Herding dogs are programmed to round things up, even the children. Beagles sniff and want to run in a pack with other dogs. Labs want to carry your socks around. Dachshunds, bred to chase badgers into the ground, will burrow under your covers and into your laundry basket. Often we get grumpy when dogs do things that just come naturally. In fact, many pups and dogs are discarded simply because they did what their genes told them. It is not fair to expect a dog to become a different being when we bring them into our home.

I often caution folks to consider what a breed was developed to do before they make a decision to bring a puppy home. Sooner or later hardwired behaviors will show up. For example, my

Socialization, the process of introducing your dog to the world around him, is one of the most crucial aspects of puppy raising.

Shelties frequently want to bark at the neighbor dog through the fence. This is a hardwired behavior, as the breed was created to guard farmyards from invaders.

Naturally, the hardwiring for some dogs is easier to live with than others. Dogs bred specifically as lapdogs, for example, are often easier to handle. Retrieving breeds are often strongly programmed to look to their trainer for direction. The popularity of the Labrador and Golden Retriever reflects the relative ease of training this type of dog.

If you love a particular breed, go for it—as long as you are realistic about the specific training issues you are likely to encounter.

Dogs are hardwired for certain behaviors. The Dachshund, for example, bred to chase badgers into the ground, will burrow under the covers.

Implications for Puppy Raising

Good trainers learn to teach around or accommodate hardwired breed-specific behaviors, but they know that they cannot make them disappear. For example, sighthounds will want to run for the horizon, particularly if a small animal catches their attention. It is imperative as you work with your pup that you consider his hardwired behaviors. This in no way implies that he can't be trained, but it will help you think about how to manage those behaviors. For example, your sighthound may need to stay on a long leash in open areas. Barking dogs like my Shelties may not be able to have free access to a backyard unless I am there to monitor, since they could easily annoy the neighbors.

General Dog Behaviors

In addition to hardwired, breed-specific behaviors, there are three aspects of canine behavior that extend across all breeds: digging, chewing, and a need to move. Modern dogs are descended from ancestors that ran and hunted for hours, buried food to keep it handy for a snack, and used their teeth to rip muscle and chew bone.

Dog owners often learn about these behaviors the hard way. When I was a youngster with my first dog, I came home to find a large section of drywall had been removed from the wall in my rental. Leaving an active dog alone for several hours seems silly to me now. I try to remember my experience when puppy raisers tell me that their pup destroyed several kitchen cabinets or turned the leather sofa into a chew toy while left loose and alone for several hours. In her book *Culture Clash*, author Jean Donaldson says it best when she writes of the dog's world that "it's all chew toys to them."

Implications for Puppy Raising

Our pups and dogs are more contented and better behaved when we find a way to meet their hardwired needs. For example, savvy trainers with pups who have a strong drive to dig often set up a digging area in their yard. They bury safe treats and let the pup go at it. Because the dog has a reason to dig there, digging in other places is often diminished.

One of the issues many puppy raisers seem to find challenging is providing adequate exercise for pups hardwired to run long distances. Many behavioral problems arise because certain pups have excess energy and try to entertain themselves in ways we wish they wouldn't. This is particularly common with herding breeds that originally worked full days keeping livestock in line. Consider that a healthy, conditioned Border Collie can run 50 miles (80.5 km) a day. Puppy raisers with high-energy dogs must be amazingly creative about wearing their pups out physically and mentally or give up and buy a small ranch. Otherwise, there will be unattractive consequences.

Common hardwired canine behaviors include digging and chewing.

Provide your dog with sufficient exercise to keep him healthy and out of trouble.

One important note is that resorting to punishment never works for hardwired behaviors. You will need to be a problem solver and think of solutions for pups who are driven to dig, chew, and run.

No Conscience

You may need to sit down for this one. This difference between dogs and humans often generates an argument. Here it is: Dogs do not have a conscience. A conscience requires the ability to think through the implications of something you are about to do. Dog brains cannot do this. Imagine the following scenario:

You leave your pup and go out to do errands. He would like to go in the car with you, but you think the car would get too warm, so you tell him to be a good boy and leave, giving him the run of your deck. As your car pulls away, he feels anxious. He looks out the fence, wanders for a bit, and then climbs up on the chaise lounge where you often relax. He nuzzles the chaise pillow. It is filled with your smell. He licks it several times and then starts chewing on the corner. Chewing always calms him down. Finally, he is relaxed enough to take a nap. An hour later you come in and see him surrounded by the plastic covering of the pillow and billows of stuffing. You wake him up yelling, "You *know* better!" He leaps off the furniture and races as far away as he can. You think he looks guilty. "What a *bad* dog you are," you add to make your point. He turns away. He is afraid of your expression and loud voice. He has no idea why you are so upset.

Remember that pups and dogs will do what meets their needs at the moment. This is a huge and immensely important concept. If your dog is bored and lonely, and tearing the siding off the house takes the edge off those feelings, he will tear the siding off the house.

Implications for Puppy Raising

It is your job as the big brain to figure out how to organize your dog's life so that he doesn't have a chance or the energy to misbehave. It is impossible to be perfect, but you can come very close.

There are three implications. First, when your pup does something destructive, recognize it for what it is: your mistake. When Scout was a baby, she chewed the corner off a coffee table when she managed to slide her exercise pen close to the table while I was out. Naturally, I was not happy. I had not planned to have a distressed table quite so soon, but I knew it was my fault. I did not expect her to feel bad and she definitely did not. Second, use your crate and exercise pen to keep your pup safe when you need to go out. Oh, yes, keep it far enough away from the furniture. While your pup is in his crate or pen, give him plenty to do, such as chew on a durable toy. In general, leave him alone for no more than four hours at a time. Lastly, provide enough exercise for your pup. A tired pup does not get in nearly as much trouble as one with lots of energy. Nothing wears a pup out more than a ten-minute training session followed by an intense play session.

In Conclusion

Although pups are smart critters and share some traits with us, they are not people. It is actually lovely that they aren't. It spares us all the complexities of interacting with people. It allows us to share a pure, uncomplicated love.

I was with my veterinarian recently, and we were trying to figure out why Scout was limping. Since we were a bit baffled, the veterinarian said, "It would be great if she could talk for just a minute." Then we looked at each other and said in unison, "Maybe not." We both laughed, knowing exactly what we meant.

Use a crate or exercise pen to keep your puppy safe when you need to go out.

Chapter 4
Top 10
Training Secrets

I watch television shows about dog training compulsively. I am fascinated by the way the programs are organized. Somehow the producers find someone who has a completely out-of-control dog. He growls when asked to get off the sofa or drags the owner face down on the sidewalk when walking to the park. The owner is completely clueless. Then a super trainer swoops in and fixes the problem in a few lessons. There is great adulation, as if something miraculous has just taken place.

The implication from these shows is that there are Super Trainers who have some extraordinary genetic prowess. Pshaw. Virtually anyone who is willing to learn can become a competent dog trainer. It is easier for some than others, but it is within everyone's grasp. I have worked with dozens of novice trainers who have never even had a dog who became

Luring involves using a bit of food to get a dog to choose a behavior you want.

lovely puppy teachers in a year. These folks were not extraordinary. They simply learned ten important rules that apply to teaching pups and then put them into action.

If you are new to training, don't panic as you read these guidelines. There is no need to memorize them. All of these "secrets" are embedded in the exercises that follow. I will remind you about them on occasion. By the time you finish this book, you will be able to chat about dog training like a pro at your next cocktail party.

Rule #1: Motivate Your Dog to Choose Desired Behavior

Teaching humans and pups is always most effective when the "student" chooses a certain behavior because he learns that doing it pays off. Let's look at a simple example. Imagine that you want your pup to learn to lie down. If you hold a bit of food on the ground near the pup's feet, he will try to figure out how to get it. He may try different behaviors. If you just continue holding the food in the same place, he will eventually try lying down on his own. If you release the food the minute he drops his belly to the floor, you effectively communicate that lying down pays off. Repeat this game a number of times and the pup begins to think that lying down is cool.

For every command or game that you want to teach your pup, it is your job to figure out what would give him a good reason to do that. Want him to piddle outside? Then you have to figure out what makes going outside more worthwhile than squatting inside. Want him to greet guests nicely when they enter your house? Then your job as his teacher is to figure out what will give him a better reason to sit quietly than leaping on new arrivals.

In this book, we will often use a strategy called luring to get the pup to choose a behavior. Luring involves using a bit of food to get the pup to choose to do something you want. In the example above, the trainer lured the pup into the *down*. It is equally easy to teach a pup to sit by lifting a tidbit from nose to forehead. The puppy's head goes up and his bottom goes down. Then you can tell your pup what a good fellow he is. Luring is just a starting point to training. You can drop the lure as soon as the pup gets an idea what you are asking. Some trainers see luring as cheating in some way. My experience is that luring is a humane teaching method that works fairly quickly. I have worked with hundreds of dogs who were lured initially when learning a new command and went on to become eager workers without being dependent on food.

Rule #2: Use Positive Methods

Dog training has undergone a revolution in recent years. Positive training methods now provide an alternative to correction-based training. People have trained for many years using choke collars,

Teach your pup with a confident attitude.

but many of us have traded them in for clickers. Clickers create a positive association for pups in between performing specific behaviors and getting rewarded. Pups will repeat behaviors that pay off for them, and this process makes it possible to train most pups without causing them any pain.

In the next chapter, we'll explore the use of clickers and how they are used. For now, it will suffice to say that positive training using this powerful tool can be used for everything from housetraining to the highest levels of obedience competition.

Rule #3: Teach Your Pup Confidently

Earlier we discussed how you are your pup's leader and that leadership comes with some responsibilities. One of those is to teach your pup with

A kindly correction must never cause pain or fear.

a confident attitude. This is important because pups need to respect the boss and know that things are under control in order to relax.

Even if you are new to raising a pup, it is important that you approach formal lessons and informal interactions around the house with confidence. If you don't convey that you are in charge, your pup will be anxious at best and may challenge your authority at worst.

After I had left the classroom to become a middle school principal, I noticed that it was common for a child to behave very well in one classroom and behave very badly in another. The difference was that one teacher was sure of herself, had clear expectations, and provided the perfect balance of pressure to learn and support. The other teacher was unconvincing and communicated weakness.

In the same vein, pups often behave entirely differently for two puppy raisers in the same house. Recently, an adolescent pup in my classes was a model citizen for one family member but bouncing off the other's back as if she were a trampoline. The solution was easy: The human trampoline needed to get some attitude.

When I work with novice puppy raisers who need to build their confidence, we focus on using a firm (but friendly) tone of voice, erect posture, giving clear directions about what is okay and what isn't, and using a kindly correction if it is called for. I often joke that puppy raising is as much about leadership training as it is about raising a pup.

Once you understand this, go back and watch one of the television trainer shows. What you will notice is that every one of the owners of the out-of-control dogs lacks confidence with their dogs. Their dogs are confused and often afraid.

Rule #4: Use Kindly Corrections Only When Necessary

There are always moments in puppy raising when you need to tell your pup in a kindly but firm way that his behavior is unacceptable. Anyone who says that you will never need to lay down the law with your dog is fooling you.

The kindly correction is intended to tell the dog that he needs to stop something he is doing. Earlier I mentioned how Shelties are hardwired to bark to guard the "farmyard." Yelling at barking dogs never helps, so when my Sheltie pups are young, I frequently toss an empty can with a few coins taped inside toward a pup who is barking at the fence at imaginary invaders. The noise is just enough to startle and quiet the pup. Then I provide a different activity to distract him and keep him busy.

A kindly correction must never cause pain or fear. In fact, the more that you can make the correction appear to happen independently of you, the more powerful it is. Tossing the coin-loaded can is powerful because the pup has no idea where it comes from.

If at any time your pup shows a fear response when you are working together, your corrections have gone beyond being kind. This will damage your relationship with your pup.

Play is an excellent way to reinforce your dog for a behavior that you like.

Rule #5: Control Your Pup's Resources

A resource is something an animal or human values. Earlier I mentioned that by controlling those resources with your pup, you automatically become his leader without trying at all. Generally, puppy resources are food, toys, play, and interactions with you. It is your job as your puppy's teacher to find out what lights your puppy up and then use these resources strategically to help him learn.

Food

As you've read, food is your most powerful resource. I recommend that for the first month, your pup receive all his food—regular meals and treats—directly from you. You can simply hand-feed him, which teaches him that you are the source of all goodness. In addition, you will use much of his food ration during the short training sessions we will discuss in this book.

Although you want your new dog to get along with other dogs in the house, it's important that he bond most closely with you.

Toys

Toys are also an important resource. Many puppy raisers overlook this and lavish dozens of toys on their pups without asking anything of them. It is better to save special toys that the pup gets only when he plays with you. For example, a cloth flying disc might be a special toy that you bring out only to teach your pup to retrieve.

Play

Play is also an excellent way to reinforce a dog for a behavior that you like. It also teaches your pup to play interactively with you rather than playing alone or with other dogs. For example, my youngest Sheltie loves it when I throw myself down on the ground and let him kiss my face after he has trained for a few minutes. This might not work with a Mastiff pup, but you can find a game he loves. Games should not involve letting the pup mouth you, of course, and you need to stop, as you would with a child, before the pup gets excessively wound up.

Interactions

The fourth resource is a bit different. It involves controlling your pup's interactions. If you have other dogs, it is possible that your pup may bond more closely with another dog than with you unless you control this resource. It is important that a new pup in the household has adequate time alone with you without another dog. Make sure that your pup goes on lots of field trips just with you, hangs out with you, and has training sessions alone. I have worked with a number of people whose dogs were anxious when separated from another dog. This is not necessary if a pup develops his own identity from the first day at your house.

Rule #6: Reinforce Your Pup Strategically

Controlling your pup's resources is important. The next step is learning to use those resources to reinforce your pup for learning what you are asking.

Technically speaking, when you provide some resource to your pup during training in the hopes that he will repeat a behavior, it is called "reinforcement." The more the pup associates the reinforcement with the thing he did, the more likely it is that he will repeat that behavior. I will use this word and the word "reward" interchangeably because the difference seems too subtle to worry about.

Reinforcement is easy to understand. It is something that increases the odds that we will repeat a behavior. Winning a ribbon in a dog show is reinforcement that raises the odds I will enter another show. Getting a paycheck at work raises the odds that I will return to work the next day. Cookies, play, and praise reinforce pup behaviors if used correctly. It is important to remember that an item reinforces a behavior only if the item is valued by the recipient. For example, I like chocolate. I do not like oranges. If you gave me a bit of chocolate every time I sat on our green sofa, I would like sitting there a lot. If you gave me an orange several times, I would steer clear of the sofa. As soon as you bring your pup home, observe what he values so that you can use that in teaching him.

Reinforcement is a well-researched topic. For those of you who would like to delve more deeply, author Karen Pryor wrote a classic book titled *Don't Shoot the Dog!* in which she details the world of reinforcement. When and where you deliver those resources to your pup is immensely important in determining how much and how fast he will learn. Let's look at a few key guidelines.

Human foods, such as chopped-up hot dog slices, usually have the highest value for pups.

Reinforcement Value

Resources that you can use in teaching your pup have different values. Dry food is generally lowest in value. Human food such as chopped chicken bits is usually the highest-value.

In the beginning, your pup should get a treat for almost every successful training effort.

Use low-value treats to reinforce behaviors that are easy for your pup or that he has known for a long time. Save the high-value stuff for teaching behaviors that are more challenging. A toy kept just for training may be of high value depending on your pup's preferences. Petting has different values for different pups. As you train your dog, you may find it useful to keep a list of items that motivate him and rank them in value. In our house, the reward items ranked from lowest to highest are:

- toasted oat cereal
- petting
- falling on the ground for a kiss fest
- a piece of dry dog food
- toy play with a ball, tug toy with rabbit fur, or cloth flying disc
- commercial dog food treats
- hot dog or chicken bits
- homemade treats such as tuna brownies

Availability and Timing

Unlike people, who learn to wait for reinforcements such as a paycheck, pups need to get their reward immediately following the behavior. Once more than five seconds go by, the pup has no idea why he is getting that cookie.

This means that when you are training a pup, you need to have food everywhere so that you can reinforce immediately for appropriate behaviors. To teach your pup to come every time you call, keep small bowls of toasted oat cereal all over the house and reinforce him every time he comes. I don't put the treat bowls away until the pup turns at least a year old. In addition, keep small treats in your pockets for immediate reinforcement. If your pup piddles outside and you have to run inside to get a treat, the moment has been lost.

When to Reinforce

When you are starting to teach your pup any new behavior, the rate of reinforcement should be very high. That means that the pups should get a treat for almost every effort. I am always exhorting puppy raisers to be generous with their treats if the pup is doing something right. For example, if your eight-week-old pup sits, pop a treat in his mouth. This is the primary way to tell him that you like it when he does that.

Once your pup has plenty of experience with a behavior, it's time to start reinforcing in one of two different ways. If you continue to reinforce 100 percent of the time, your pup will get to thinking that he doesn't have to put out much effort: *Hey, those treats just keep coming.* You might switch to what is called "fixed reinforcement." This means that you deliver your treats in a fixed pattern such as every other *sit* or every third *sit*. Another option is to go to "variable

Make puppy teaching sessions short and lighthearted so that you can keep his attention.

reinforcement." This means that you follow a random pattern. For example, you might treat twice for a *sit*, skip once, treat once, skip twice. Either of these methods encourages the pup to try harder to do what you want because he wants to earn one of those goodies. As your pup matures, you will space out the treats even further but continue to praise every good effort.

Where to Reinforce

Where you reinforce your pup is of immense importance. Try very hard to deliver your treat when he is still doing the behavior that earned him the cookie. For example, when you are teaching your pup to walk next to you, he needs to receive his treat when his ear is right against your knee. If when he walks ahead of you, you reach out to reward him, you are teaching him that walking ahead of you is okay. When you are teaching *sit*, deliver the cookie while he is still seated. Reinforce for *down* while your pup is still prone.

Be Mindful

In puppy class, I often see puppy raisers popping treats into their pup's mouth, but I can't identify what they are reinforcing. When I ask what they were rewarding, they smile sheepishly. Try to be mindful that each time you reinforce your pup, you should have some specific behavior in mind.

Rule #7: Make Training Sessions a Joy for Your Pup (and You)

In this book, I will frequently use the word "work" when I refer to training sessions with your pup. I want to be very clear that work does not mean that the session has to be serious. It would be better to call it "workfun." As you plan for teaching sessions with your pup, emphasize workfun by the way you structure lessons and how you interact with your pup during those lessons.

Keep Sessions Short and Sweet

For starters, make puppy teaching sessions short and lighthearted. Pups, like children, have a short attention span. For pups younger than four months, five minutes at a time is plenty. It is best to do several short sessions a day if your schedule allows. As your pup matures, you can add a few minutes, but short sessions focused on just one or two games or skills are better than longer sessions with too many exercises.

If you sign up for a puppy class, most of which go at least an hour, make sure to plan for puppy breaks. When the teacher is talking or when your pup is waiting his turn to practice a game, give him a chew toy. Most pups settle down and relax with the chew, which is restful physically and mentally. If you forget a chewie or if your pup is obviously tired, sit on the floor and cradle him to break up the time. There is an exercise in Chapter 7: Relationship Building that explains the details of cradling.

Work/Play Balance

Second, alternate teaching and playing during every lesson. I often say in class that pups shouldn't really know whether they are learning or playing. Most pups turn off if asked to do things over and over. In general, three repetitions of one command at a time are enough.

Positive Attitude

The final aspect of making training fun for your pup relates directly to you. I have observed hundreds of puppy raisers. Most raise well-behaved, pleasant dogs. A few raise dogs who are joyous. They just bounce and smile as they work. Naturally, genes play a part in this, but there is more. When I closely observe these joyful teams, I notice that the handlers of these pups:

A positive attitude on your part will help you raise a well-behaved, joyous pup.

- smile at their dogs a lot
- laugh frequently
- walk with a spring in their step
- talk to their pups in a high, happy voice
- are fearless about appearing silly

Working with your pup is a great time to let down your hair. No one will ever be as nonjudgmental as your canine pal. Relax and have fun while you work and play together. Figure out what amuses and delights your pup and use it to teach him.

Rule #8: Strive for Consistency

No puppy training book would be worth its salt if it didn't mention the importance of consistency. This is another one of those concepts that make puppy raisers nod as if it is obvious. Then, after practicing heeling in class, they let their pup drag them to the car. I weep quietly as I watch, knowing that this inconsistency results in a pup with no idea what *heel* means.

Consistency in teaching our pups is one of the most challenging aspects of puppy raising. It takes a good deal of thinking and planning. There are two aspects of consistency to consider:

1. Once you begin teaching a pup a behavior, you must ask for that behavior all the time. The example above in which the pup drags his owner to the car is a classic case of changing the rules. Pups have no way to process this inconsistency. Author Dale Stavroff writes that if a pup breaks a rule one out of ten times, there is no rule. This is so true.
2. Consistency around the house is an equally important issue. Some challenges rear their head with multiple family members. One person lets the pup on the sofa. The other freaks out. One lets the pup leap up on guests when they arrive. The other insists that the pup lie down

Consistency when training is important—one person in the household can't allow the dog on the couch when another family member doesn't allow it, for example.

while company enters. One person roughhouses and lets the puppy nip. The other corrects him for mouthing. These conflicting rules are impossible for pups or dogs to understand. If possible, sit down with your family to discuss the rules for your pup before he arrives and then assign someone in the family the job of watching for consistency.

Rule #9: Gradually Increase Distractions

This rule is a cousin to the previous one and highlights the process by which dogs learn to generalize so that they can behave either at a friend's house or when watching a town parade complete with horses, marching bands, and people in costumes.

To accomplish this, your formal training should follow a specific progression. Always start each new teaching word at your home. Your pup shouldn't be distracted by anything unusual. Teach the command there until he responds to your direction consistently. Then take him somewhere a bit more distracting and work on it again. For my pups, this means we move from the backyard to the front sidewalk. When my dog is able to respond there, as cars and neighbors pass, we go to the strip mall nearby. I work the pup in a quiet aisle. When he performs well there, we move in front of the grocery with lots of traffic and rattling carts. When he ignores that to play our training games with me, we are off to the downtown area.

If at any time your pup is unable to perform an exercise that he "knew" before, you have likely moved too far too fast. Go back to the previous level of distraction until he regains his confidence and then find a setting that is just a bit more stimulating.

Rule #10: Become a Problem Solver

Pups and dogs are as individual as children. Some pups are eager to learn, while others are distracted by anything going on. Some pups are "soft" and stressed by new experiences, while others are confident and independent. As a result, pups do unexpected things.

The best puppy trainers are amazing problem solvers. They understand that there is always some strategy to teach their pup what they want. Rather than trying harder with an approach that isn't working, these teachers get creative and find a way to teach their pup so that he is successful. It is the problem-solving aspect of teaching pups that keeps it interesting.

I will share a very embarrassing story to highlight the importance of creativity. My youngest Sheltie got confused when he was a pup and thought that he was supposed to poop on an entry carpet at the front door. Go figure. I was horrified and wanted to berate him, but I could tell by his consistent behavior that he thought it was the right thing to do. I decided to gradually move the carpet across the house and then outside. It took almost three weeks. I left it on the patio for another week and then moved it onto the grass. Finally, I cut the carpet off by small chunks. The fourth week he was doing his best to go on a square the size of a playing card. Then it went away too. Problem solved. For most things your pup might try, there is a kind solution. If you can't come up with any ideas, brainstorm with your dog friends.

In Conclusion

Now that you know the inside secrets of training pros, take a break and watch a television training show. You will find that you can identify each of these guidelines that the trainer is putting into action. You may even feel smug: *Look at those people. They have given that dog no reason to stop pulling.* With that understanding, you are almost ready to launch your own career as a Super Trainer of a gifted pup. Let's just explore how you can use a clicker and other equipment to help you reach that goal.

Start training each new command at home to prevent your pup from becoming distracted.

Chapter 5
To Click or Not to Click

A clicker is a small noisemaker that precisely marks a desired behavior.

There has been a substantial shift away from traditional dog training based on correcting undesired behaviors and toward positive dog training in which desired behaviors are reinforced. The positive approach that I use and advocate is called clicker training.

In clicker training, first we get the pup to do a behavior we want. We discussed luring as an appropriate strategy to do that. Next we use a small noisemaker that tells the dog we like what he did. Lastly, we reinforce the behavior with something the dog values, such as a cookie. (When I say to deliver a "cookie" I am picturing a tiny corner of a biscuit.) For example, if you have a tiny pup, you might lure him into a sitting position, click as soon as his bottom hits the ground, and then pop a treat in his mouth a couple of seconds later. As you remember, rewarding a pup for a behavior increases the odds that he will repeat the behavior. Personally, if you gave me a molasses chip every time I sat down, I would wear myself out sitting. Your pup will do the same once he understands this game.

How the Clicker Works

At the heart of clicker training is a clicking device that trainers use to communicate clearly. Clickers come in a variety of colors and shapes these days. Most dog supply stores and training websites have them available. Most clickers make a quick snapping noise, but there are newer versions programmed to make a variety of sounds, including a bird chirp.

The clicker is more effective than verbal praise because the sound is quicker, and it can consistently highlight a specific behavior. Many puppy raisers prefer to say, "Good dog," when a pup does something they want. For most pups, the verbal affirmation is not as powerful a communication as the clicker because they have been good-dogged (hopefully) from dawn to dark. The clicker is more powerful because it stands out from all the other sounds that the pup hears all day.

The noise made by the clicker is technically known as a "mark" because it marks exactly what the trainer liked. For example, if you ask your dog to sit and you give a well-timed click that marks the exact moment his rear hits the ground, it leaves little doubt in the dog's mind what you wanted and that he got it right. The treat that follows the click solidifies the learning.

I have fallen in love with clicker training for three simple reasons. The clicker gives me a special language with my dogs, and it is a language that makes them happy. Pups quickly understand that the click means the equivalent of "Bingo!" As a result, they are joyful every time they hear the sound. They become so eager to learn that they offer different behaviors hoping to earn that wonderful sound. Second, the clicker allows me to teach my dogs without hurting or scaring them.

Our training sessions build rather than damage our relationship. Third, I can tell my pups I like what they have just done from a distance. For example, if my pup runs across the family room and into his kennel, I can click to tell him I like that even though I am watching from the kitchen. Naturally, I have to walk to the kennel after I click to deliver a treat, but I can stroll over since my pup knows I am good for it.

Most high-level animal training is done using the clicker. Assistance dogs who learn to turn lights on and off, open refrigerators, and push drawers shut are taught by trainers who click to tell them they are doing a fine job. Performing whales and dolphins are taught with this method—although a whistle replaces the click because it can be heard underwater. Don't underestimate the power of this seemingly humble little tool.

Learning to Use the Clicker

Some of you may have already discovered how to use the clicker to teach dogs without resorting to

The clicker allows you to positively reinforce a behavior even from a distance, such as when your pup comes to you.

corrections or coercion. For those of you who are just discovering this method, many local dog clubs now offer classes in clicker training. If a class is not available, I will provide you with plenty of step-by-step guidelines in Part II.

The biggest challenge of clicker training is learning to time the click to the exact moment the pup does what you want. A late click might mean that you mark something you didn't intend. It is fun to practice your timing with friends. In our puppy classes, I sit and stand several times. My students do their best to click each time my bottom hits the seat.

Remember that when you are going to use your clicker, you must always have food with you, because every click results in a treat. Keep the treats tiny so that your pup doesn't get filled up.

The clicker can be used in

The clicker can be used very effectively if you plan to train your dog for a performance sport like agility.

innumerable ways. If you plan to train your pup for a performance sport such as rally, obedience, or agility, clicker training has become the gold standard. Throughout this book, I will teach you dozens of ways to use your clicker. By the time you finish, you will be able to think of many more.

As I mentioned in an earlier chapter, I am not a purist. I do find rare occasions when pups need to get told gently and firmly to knock a behavior off. For example, the clicker isn't effective for teaching a pup not to hurt you with his teeth when he takes a training treat out of your hand. Rather, you should squeal in pain when he bites you, a sound that pups recognize as meaning something hurts.

Key Clicker Principles

There are five basic principles to remember in clicker training:
1. Initially, the clicking sound has no meaning to your pup. You must teach him (known as "conditioning") that the click is a positive thing with a clear message: I like what you did and something good is going to happen.

2. You can only use the clicker for one specific behavior at a time.
3. The effectiveness of the clicker is all about timing. Work to perfect your method so that you click exactly at the moment the dog does what you want. The click is a marker for the exact behavior you are asking for. If you click late, your dog will associate the click with whatever he happened to be doing at the time of the click.
4. The clicker implies that you have a contract with your dog. What that contract says is that if you click, your dog is guaranteed a cookie. Guaranteed. If you don't deliver, your dog will come to mistrust the click and the clicker will lose its power as a training tool. So even if you click by mistake, and trust me, you will, you must reward your dog. It won't ruin him to get an occasional freebie.
5. The reinforcement you give after the click must be a high-value reward—ideally food. If your dog loves dry food, that will work. If not, you need to use a higher-powered treat. If your dog loves games, you can also substitute a quick play period such as tug. You can also use praise and petting if those are high value for your pup.

Earlier I mentioned that play and petting can be used in addition to food to reinforce a puppy. This is definitely true. However, if you are new to clicker training, it is best to use food as described. This allows you to reward your pup *while* he is doing what you asked rather than reinforcing him for getting up to play with you. Use play and physical contact to reinforce your pup when you are teaching him without the clicker.

Must I Use a Clicker?

Now and then, a student tells me that she doesn't want to use the clicker. She feels that she doesn't have enough hands to handle the dog, treats, leash, and the clicker. Before you give up, I suggest buying a clicker with a stretchy wristband. Without the band, I frequently drop or misplace my clicker.

If you try the clicker and simply can't manage it, you can substitute a word such as "yes!" for the click. However, it is very difficult to

The clicker implies that you have a contract with your dog—if you click, your dog gets a treat.

be as precise with your voice as you can be with this lovely little tool. Training with a clicker is simply more efficient because any word has a tendency to disappear into the torrent of our other words, while the sound of the clicker is unique. A word used in place of a clicker is known as a "marker." Throughout this book, I will highlight opportunities to use your clicker. If you are choosing to use a marker instead, simply substitute it where I say to click.

When to Leave the Clicker Behind

There are also games and exercises that are not appropriate for the clicker. These are generally activities where the pup's behavior makes it hard to hold the clicker or it would be hard to know exactly when to click. In these cases, it is better just to use your voice to verbally praise your dog and then reward. For example, I'll introduce you to a game in which you teach your pup to weave back and forth through your legs. Since you will start by holding a treat in each hand, it is difficult to manage the clicker too. In each of the exercises in this book, I will suggest whether it is best to use the clicker or not.

Misuses of the Clicker

Let me start by saying that the clicker is a communication tool. It is not a tool for getting a pup to initiate a specific behavior. You can imagine my surprise when a

The reinforcement you give after the click must be a high-value reward, ideally food.

new student came to class recently and said that she was clicking when she wanted her dog to come. This would work, of course, since words and sounds are all the same to dogs. However, the problem was that she no longer could use the clicker to tell her pup that she liked it when he came to her. You can avoid similar mistakes by remembering that the click always happens *during* the pup's behavior. It never gets the pup to start a behavior.

A second misuse of the clicker is based on a misunderstanding. Sometimes I see trainers click after the pup has done a complex trick. This rewards the dog for whatever he is doing at that moment but doesn't relate to the trick at all in the dog's mind. For example, if I click one of my agility dogs over the last jump when he has run a full course, it tells him that I like the way he did that jump but it doesn't tell him that I liked any other part of what he did.

Both of these issues can be easily avoided. When you click, you should always have a clear reason in your mind. Try to prepare mentally about why and when you are clicking a behavior. Never use the clicker to tell your pup in a general sense that he is a fine guy.

The clicker should be used *while* a pup performs the desired behavior, not after it occurs.

When the Clicker Won't Work

There is one limitation with the clicker. It won't work if your pup doesn't value food tidbits. The clicker's power lies in the dog understanding that his specific behaviors can earn him food.

If you manage your pup's resources as we discussed and use your pup's meals for training, you can often convince a pup that eating is a good idea. Bring out your highest-value cookies to get him started.

In Conclusion

It is possible to raise a gifted pup without a clicker. On the other hand, if you choose to use the clicker, you may well find it the best few dollars you've ever spent. Used well, it will accelerate your pup's learning and allow you to communicate with him more clearly than you ever imagined possible.

Chapter 6
Equipment Matters

Recently, a woman brought a powerful Lab-cross pup to class using a flat collar. Whenever this guy caught a whiff of something, he dragged her around like a bit of flotsam. We switched this fellow to one of the new no-pull harnesses. With a bit of practice, he quit pulling within a week because it no longer paid off for him. This did not mean that the woman's pup was trained, but it did mean that she could get his attention to start training.

Equipment sounds like such a dry topic. In reality, it's not. In fact, it is an area fraught with controversy among trainers, all of whom have strong feelings about what is best to use. I am no different. My prejudices will shine through clearly in this chapter.

Perhaps the most interesting thing about puppy training equipment is that it is not perfect. You would think that after our long history with canines, we would we have hit on the ideal tools for managing pups. Whatever you choose to use with your pup will have distinct pro and con columns. I will provide that information for you and then you may need to do a bit of experimenting to find the best match for your pup.

The right equipment will help make training your dog a lot easier.

There are five things you will need to select:

1. The equipment you use to connect you to your pup, such as a buckle collar or a head halter
2. Your leashes
3. A long line
4. A bag for your training tools, such as your clicker and treats
5. A crate and/or exercise pen

Connecting to Your Dog

The devices for controlling your pup while you teach him to be a good canine citizen cover a full spectrum, from the traditional flat collar to some intimidating metal collars. We will start with the two newest options and then consider the more traditional choices.

Head-Type Halter

Recently, dog trainers have adapted the technology used on horses for years. The head-type halter fits around the dog's nose and fastens behind his head, just below his ears. It works the same as a halter works on a horse, by controlling the head. Many folks who first see the head halter mistake it as a muzzle of some sort. In fact, it does not restrict the dog's mouth from opening at all. Your pup can pant, drink water, and even eat with his head halter on. Naturally, a pup should always be supervised when wearing this device.

This type of equipment is an excellent, humane training tool. It simply makes pulling unattractive to a puppy because it pulls his head down and back if he forges ahead. It is important not to jerk on the head halter at all since this could cause a neck injury, and it should never be used with an expanding leash where the pup might bolt ahead.

The head halter should be carefully fitted. The band that fastens on the pup's neck should ride high, just below the ears, and you should be able to slide one finger under the band. The band around the nose should be tightened just so that it can't slide off the pup's nose. It should never touch your pup's eyes.

The head halter can be introduced to a puppy as young as eight weeks. The introduction should be very slow and may take two or three weeks. Make sure that the pup is never unsupervised and allowed to paw the head halter off because this will teach him to try this regularly.

The drawbacks of the head-type halter are threefold:

1. Most but not all puppies tolerate it. Even when introduced to the device very slowly, some pups are clearly unhappy. They obsess with trying to rub the halter off on the ground or against

Puppies with short noses, such as the Boston Terrier, may not have enough space between the eyes and nose to accommodate a head halter's nose band.

the handler's legs. Sometimes the introduction to the halter has been too fast for these babies, or sometimes they are canines who have particularly sensitive bodies. Pups who dislike the halter sometimes get used to it and others never give up the battle. I would not give up too quickly.

2. Next, puppies with short noses such as Boston Terriers or Mastiffs may not have enough space between the eyes and nose to accommodate the nose band.

3. The biggest issue may be that pups trained in a head-type halter often have no idea how to behave when the device is not on. We deal with this frequently with the Canine Companions pups, all of whom are trained in the head-type halter. If you choose this device, it is important that you also work on skills such as walking nicely on the leash when the head halter is off.

If you choose to use a head halter, you should also work on skills like walking nicely on leash when the head halter is off.

No-Pull Harness

The latest generation of harnesses provides an exciting new option. Unlike older models, the leash attaches to a ring on the pup's chest. When the pup tugs on the leash, the harness applies pressure on his shoulders. The gentle pressure discourages the pup from pulling without putting strain on his neck or head. In addition, a pup who takes off is flipped around to face the handler when he runs out of leash. The best news is that is impossible to hurt a dog with this device.

I recently used a no-pull harness to teach a young rescue Border Collie not to pull within two training sessions. I let her do the work herself. When she bolted, I just stood still. When she reached the end of the leash, the harness just turned her back to face me. When she looked at me, I invited her to come back and then rewarded her for returning and then walking next to me. She figured out very quickly that there was no payoff for running away and that walking next to me was the safest place. It was a very quick resolution of a problem, and the pup had no idea I had anything to do with it.

Harnesses come with excellent directions about fitting the pup, introducing the pup to the harness, and how to handle this tool during training and walks. I have found it useful to have knowledgeable store staff help me with harness adjustments initially. If left too large, they rotate on the dog, which minimizes some of their leverage. They come in sizes that will work for tiny Chihuahuas and giant Great Danes.

Be careful when you purchase that you don't accidentally pick up the older style of dog harness that attaches on the dog's back. There is little to recommend about these because they encourage pulling.

Martingale Leash Combo

The martingale leash combo is a newer option for training. It consists of a one-piece leash and collar. It must be adjusted to fit your particular pup's neck. When pressure is applied by pulling on the leash, the collar portion tightens. However, the leash construction stops the collar before the dog becomes too uncomfortable. For sensitive and smaller dogs, this is a good training option. This is the device I find most useful on my Shelties.

Buckle Collar

Traditionally, a buckle collar has generally been kept on puppies and dogs for identification purposes. Then trainers put a different collar on for training. Recently, many trainers are working more with their pups in the buckle collar. This is because this collar, properly fitted, rarely causes the puppy any pain.

If you are new to training pups, I would recommend that you use one of the other devices for teaching your pup initially because they will give you considerably more control. Then work the pup on the same game using just the buckle collar.

There will be times when you need your dog to behave on the buckle collar simply because it is all you have available. In addition, in some dog sports, such as agility, a buckle collar is the only type used during training.

Choke and Prong Collars

Finally, we arrive at the most controversial devices: choke collars and prong collars. Choke collars consist of a single strand of metal links that tighten when pulled until they literally choke the dog. The prong collar consists of a series of links, each with a

In some dog sports, a buckle collar is the only type used during training.

metal prong that pinches a dog's neck when pressure is applied. Interestingly, the choke collar presents the greatest danger to pups and dogs.

In the past, the choke collar was used in virtually every training class. The problem is that, in the hands of an inexperienced trainer, the choke can seriously hurt even a grown dog by crushing his larynx. Of equal importance, the intent of the choke collar was to startle or cause the dog a bit of pain. It took a long time for beliefs to change, but finally many trainers realized that they didn't need to hurt their dogs to get any behavior they wanted. If that isn't enough reason to give up this device, the choke collar is also very dangerous if left on an unsupervised dog, who might get choked by the collar.

The prong collar, for all its appearance as a medieval torture device, only tightens so much, so the dog can't be choked. I would suggest its use *only* if the handler is in danger of being pulled down and injured. In some cases, the prong collar has allowed some puppy raisers to keep a strong animal who was otherwise headed for rescue. Before using the collar, the prongs should be adjusted to touch but not poke into the dog's neck. If you think that you need to use this type of collar, I strongly recommend that you get it fitted by a professional trainer and that you work together to use it humanely.

Leashing Your Pup

Next, you need a leash for walks and teaching. I've noticed that inexpensive nylon leashes really burn if they are pulled through my hand. A leather leash ages well and is much kinder to your palms.

Most leashes are 6 feet (2 m) in length, but you may find it useful for some activities, such as heeling, to use a shorter leash. Something 2 or 3 feet (.5 or 1 m) long has less of a tendency to get under your pup's legs or drag on the ground and trip you.

One device that you do not want to use for training is the spring-loaded, retractable leash. They don't allow you to "work the leash" as you will learn to do in many exercises. I sometimes use retractable

Don't use a retractable leash for training—they encourage dogs prone to pulling to run out front and take charge.

A long leash can help you teach your puppy to come to you reliably.

leashes when I take my pups on a walk along a coastal bluff, but I don't recommend them for dogs prone to pulling, because they encourage them to run out front and take charge.

The Long Line

There is another tool that is much underused in training pups, called a long line. This very light piece of rope or twine, about 15 to 30 feet (4.5 to 9 m) in length, can be found by the foot at most hardware stores. Go for the lightest weight that will hold your pup since you want him to forget that he has the line on. At the same time that you purchase the rope, buy a very light clip. Tie the clip onto the rope. Next, tie knots in the rope every 3 or 4 feet (1 or 1.2 m) so that it won't just slip through your hands.

You will be using the long line in a multitude of ways during your pup's first year in the games that follow. You will use it to teach your puppy to come to you reliably. You may use it to teach your pup to ignore food on your kitchen counter. It is a handy tool, and we will put it to full use.

Now for the Bag

As you have read in previous chapters, we are going to reinforce each of your pup's correct behaviors with tiny tidbits. Remember how long you have to deliver a treat? Five seconds. After that, the pup has no idea why he is getting a cookie.

A crate and exercise pen are excellent tools to use to keep your puppy out of trouble when you can't supervise him.

Developing a system for delivering treats is something that many novices struggle with. Students come to class in jeans so tight that they can't get a hand in that pocket, or they arrive in pants with no pockets. In the latter case, they try to train while clinging to a bag of treats. It is impossible for a pup to concentrate on what you are teaching him with a bag of treats flapping around his head.

The answer is simple: You need to use some kind of small bag that goes on your belt or around your waist when you have a jacket on. It needs to be easy to plunge your hand in to and grab a cookie. There are a number of commercial training bags available. Some have a couple of pockets, which is great—they allow you to put treats in one pocket and other supplies such as your clicker in the other.

Containing Your Pup

When your pup is at home, you need a system for keeping track of him so that he doesn't get into trouble. There are two tools that are perfect when you have a youngster in the house. The crate is the ideal place for your pup to relax and sleep when you can't watch him. Select a crate just big enough for your pup to stand up and turn around. (An overly large crate will encourage him to pee in a distant corner.) One of the activities that follows details the process of introducing your pup to the crate.

An exercise pen (a fold-out device available at most pet stores) that is easy to set up in any room is ideal for keeping tabs on your pup while he has a chew or plays with a favorite toy.

In Conclusion

Once you get your pup suited up in the appropriate equipment, your training program is off and running. You can pay attention to teaching your pup, and your pup can relax and pay attention to you. If your initial choice of training tools doesn't work like you hoped, regroup and try something else.

Keep in mind that your pup may quickly outgrow some equipment, such as the head-type halter, harness, collar, and crate. Most puppy training equipment is available in at least three sizes.

Part II
From Puppy
to Gifted Puppy

Now that you understand how dogs and puppies learn and how much you can teach them, it is time to leap into training. In Part II you will learn how to teach virtually all of the commands covered in many puppy training books and puppy classes—and then many more. But then, you are raising a gifted puppy.

You will find step-by-step instructions to teach basic relationship-building skills, as well as everyday behaviors like housetraining and nail trimming that will allow you to enjoy your puppy at home.

Next, we'll move on to socialization and confidence building for your pup. This refers to specific, systematic training that you can do to help your pup learn to handle everything he might encounter in the environment. Dogs who are not adequately socialized can grow up anxious and worried. But your gifted pup will learn to take garbage trucks, strangers, and loud noises in stride. If there is only one activity that you do with your dog from this book, Meet the Goblins is the most important because it will allow your dog to move easily and happily in the world.

Well-socialized, well-trained dogs can move easily and happily through the world.

Your dog can keep learning more throughout his life.

Now you are on a roll. In the next chapter, we will focus on skills that will elevate your pup into a model citizen. He will learn to sit quietly when he meets new people, to wait at every doorway, and to come on command when faced with tempting distractions.

We will wrap up this section with a wide variety of skills and games. Your pup will learn to jump on an exam table, stand on command, back up in a straight line, and lie quietly under a desk. He will wow your friends by throwing a high five. Mastering these activities will keep both of you busy for months and officially qualify your pup as gifted.

Many chapters ago, I wrote, "The more a puppy learns, the more he is capable of learning." Teaching your dog never needs to end. Working with him will enrich his life and yours. Remember, a good mind is a terrible thing to waste.

Chapter 7
Relationship Building

Relationship building and love are often mistaken for the same thing. While they are related, they are not identical. Love develops with little effort. On the other hand, relationship building takes time and energy. During relationship building, your pup learns to trust you and recognize that the most fun is being with and interacting with you. Everything you do to build your relationship with your puppy is like putting money in a savings account. If you take time to make these deposits along the way, any training techniques that you use will go better because you have established mutual understanding and respect. It is never too late to build a better bond with your dog.

Exercise #1: No Free Lunch

Goal: Bond with your pup by directly providing most of his food by hand.
Ideal Age to Start: 8 weeks
Groundwork: None
Clicker: No

Background

Hand-feeding your pup is important because it teaches him that you are the source of all goodness. As you may remember reading earlier, by controlling the resources you become the pack leader for your pup, which is the beginning of your partnership.

Hand-feeding your pup is important because it teaches him that you are the source of all goodness.

Real-Life Pups

Jade, a baby Border Collie owned by a close friend, didn't have a full meal in a bowl for a month after she arrived at her new home. Some food was delivered as described here, with Lauri sitting on the floor. The other half was delivered to help Jade learn the rules of the house. For example, when it became clear that Jade didn't take to the crate, Lauri regularly tossed a handful of treats into the back so that she would run in. If she heard a new noise, Lauri treated her directly from her hand so that she developed a positive association with the sound. When Lauri worked with Jade on her *sit*, the reward came right from her hand. Very quickly, this pup learned that her owner was the source of all goodness.

Process

Phase One
For at least four weeks, your pup will not have a meal in a bowl with the exception of a small amount for crate training, which you will read about in the next exercise. Otherwise every bit of food is delivered by you as a meal or as reinforcement when you are teaching your pup.
1. Plop yourself down on the floor and hold the bowl in your lap.
2. Feed your pup small handfuls at a reasonable speed. If he tries to go directly for the bowl, set it up on a table that you can reach but he can't.

Phase Two
After four weeks, you can end the hand-feeding, but you should continue to teach your pup there is nothing to fear by relinquishing something to you. It is best to start before a problem develops.
1. First, when your pup gets his food in a bowl, sit right next to him as you have been doing. Instead of hand-feeding, put your hand in the bowl. This just reminds the pup that you are no danger and he can trust you in close proximity.
2. After a couple of weeks, take your pup's bowl away while he is eating. Put something even more delicious in it and return it to him. This conveys a strong message that good things happen when the bowl leaves.
3. Lastly, let your pup eat on his own but on a regular basis walk up to him and add something very good to the mix. Continue this practice on occasion until your pup is at least a year old.
   If at any time your puppy growls or indicates he might bite when you are playing the games described here, find a good trainer to work with right away. This is not something that will fix itself. However the odds are very good that if you follow these guidelines regularly, you will have a gifted pup who understands that he can trust you around his food.
   Keep the balance of your pup's food in your pockets or readily available in bowls around the house, for both formal lessons and informal opportunities. For example, when you call your pup to come to you and he responds, make sure that you can reward him on the spot.

Possible Challenges

Some pups have trouble distinguishing between their food and your fingers; you can alert your pup that he is too rough by yelping when he puts his teeth on you. If you need stronger medicine, you can play a game in which the pup has to earn a mouthful by being gentle.

Offer your pup a handful of food. If he is rough, close your hand and turn it over. Wait a minute. Don't let him get any food if he tries by pawing or butting your hand. Once he steps away, open your hand again. If he takes the food gently, that's great. If he is still rough, close your hand again. Keep repeating the drill every time he mistakes your hand for something to eat.

Most dogs will work for food—it's a powerful resource.

Exercise #2: Frontload the Clicker

Goal: Teach your pup that the sound of a clicker means he has done exactly what you wanted and a treat will soon follow.
Ideal Age to Start: 8 weeks
Groundwork: Purchase a clicker.
Clicker: Yes

Background

In an earlier chapter you read about clicker training, a technique that has revolutionized dog training in recent years. It has won the hearts and minds of dog lovers because using force is not necessary with pups and dogs.

Clicker expert Karen Pryor writes, "Clicker training is an animal training method based on behavioral psychology that relies on marking desirable behavior and rewarding it. This clear form of communication combined with positive reinforcement is an effective and humane way to teach any animal any behavior that it is physically and mentally capable of doing."

In other words, the first challenge is how to "talk" with our pups so that they can understand. The clicker provides a means to communicate with pups.

Trainer Talk

A "resource" is anything your pup values. For most pups, food is the most powerful resource. Control your pup's food and use it strategically to teach him. This will automatically make you the head of the team, leader of the pack, queen of the mountain. Forget any temptation to dominate your pooch or to push him around.

Clicker trainers use a small noisemaker that tells the dog precisely what he did right. Once the animal realizes that this sound is a bridge between some behavior you like and some reinforcement he likes, you have a partner who will be eager to learn and happy to work with you.

Process

The first step in clicker training is teaching the dog that the click is a lovely sound and means that a treat or game will follow within seconds. This is called "frontloading."

1. To get started, simply click your clicker with your dog nearby and follow up by giving a treat. It is very important that you do not feed while you are clicking.
2. Always make sure that there is a delay of a few seconds before the treat is delivered—click, pause, feed, click, pause, feed, etc. This allows the dog to focus on the sound for a moment and what he was doing to earn the treat.
3. Repeat 10 to 12 times per session.

This is every dog's favorite part of training since he gets treats for doing nothing but hanging out with you. Do not ask for any other behaviors at this point. Use part of your pup's meals for this game, which will guarantee that he is hungry and associates the clicker with his favorite time of the day.

Repeat this process several times a day for at least a week. You will know when your pup is ready for you to use the clicker in other games because he will get excited when you merely get the clicker out. He may even lick his lips, which is a strong sign that he understands the link between the click and the reinforcement. My youngest dog, Boo, starts spinning wheelies the

Real-Life Pups

Although I am recommending that you frontload the clicker during your pup's first week, Lauri began to frontload the clicker with Baby Jade during her second week. She waited this long because the pup was nervous about unusual noises. (You will read more about this in Chapter 9.)

Once Lauri started frontloading the clicker, she kept the clicker deep in her pocket to muffle the sound. For a week, she played the frontloading game once or twice a day. This was enough for this particular pup. At the end of the week, she could tell that Jade understood the click meant something good had happened, and she was ready to use it to learn other games.

second I pull a clicker out of the drawer. He knows there is a good game in the offing and that he is master of the universe where dog games are concerned.

Possible Challenges

The primary challenge of clicker training is posed by pups who don't care much about food. For clicker training to work, the pup must think that the reward is valuable. See if you can find some type of food item your dog enjoys. String cheese and chicken bits are a big hit in our house.

A second challenge highlights our natural tendency to use language. Chatting can interfere with your pup paying attention to the meaning of the click. During this exercise, don't talk with your pup.

Exercise #3: Cradling Matters

Goal: Teach your pup to relax with you by lying on his back in your lap.
Ideal Age to Start: 8 weeks
Groundwork: None
Clicker: No

After clicking, pause for a few seconds before delivering the treat.

Background

Teaching your pup to enjoy lying on his back with you serves the important purpose of teaching him to trust you completely. With most pups, you can start by sitting on the sofa, but as the pup gets bigger, you may need to sit on the floor. For giant breeds, the window for cradling is fairly short, so get started right away. The younger you start a pup with this exercise, the greater the chance of success.

Don't confuse this activity with putting your pup on his back on the floor. This strategy has sometimes been recommended as a method of establishing dominance over a pup. In contrast, cradling is a gentle game designed to enhance your pup's trust of you.

Trainer Talk

Timelines for puppy training are both useful and dangerous. They keep us moving forward, but they also imply that we have to get something done with our pups. They can make us feel *behind*! I love Lauri and Jade's story told throughtout this book, because it illustrates the importance of doing things in an order and timeframe that makes sense to your pup. Pups are as individual as children.

Process

Phase One

1. Pick the puppy up and sit down somewhere comfortable where you can lean back.
2. Gently roll the pup onto his back with his head on your chest and his feet toward your knees. Hold him there and talk softly and confidently to him. Pet his stomach. Try not to let him up if he fusses.
3. Hold him just a few seconds and gently release him.

Phase Two

1. Sit on the floor with your legs stretched out in front of you.
2. Gently roll your tired pup over on your thighs so that his head is close to your knees and rub his exposed belly while he relaxes.

Possible Challenges

This is an exercise that is terrific with some pups, but for very assertive puppies it may pose a challenge. Some high-powered herding breeds are very resistant to lying on their back. Just follow the process above, and your pup will learn to relax. If your pup is very resistant, don't make a battle out of it, but try the exercise several times before you give up because the benefits are great.

    If you have a pup who will absolutely not cradle, play another game that encourages close physical contact. Put him right next to

Teaching your puppy to enjoy lying on his back with you shows him to trust you completely.

you with his side against yours. Drape your arm across his back. Gently tickle his belly to get him to stand. Then gently ease him into a sitting position and then back to standing.

Exercise #4: Love That Touch

Goal: Teach your pup that having his body touched by you or a new friend is pleasurable.

Ideal Age to Start: 8 weeks

Groundwork: Hopefully the pup's breeder has handled the pup extensively since the time he was little. The most responsible breeders systematically hold each pup in a litter so that they grow up accepting and enjoying physical contact.

Clicker: No

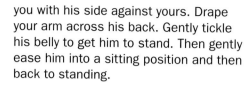

Real-Life Pups

Cristo is a young Canine Companions pup. His puppy raiser began cradling him as soon as she brought him home at eight weeks. You could see the trusting relationship they had built by the time he was ten weeks old.

Background

Some pups thrive on physical contact; others are a bit more reserved. Some pups enjoy contact on their back or belly but resist having their toes touched. The bottom line is that pups should learn to accept handling all over their body and on their collar. This is vital when you need to examine your pup, restrain him, or groom him. Most importantly, you want a pup who seeks you out for a good pat. Young Boo is the most physical dog I have ever owned. He wiggles with pleasure and moans when I rub his chest or tickle his back. While some of this is genetic, he also came from a breeder who handles her pups every day from the moment they are born.

Process

Phase One

1. Load your pocket up with small treats. Find a nice place to sit with your pup on a short leash. It is fine to sit on the floor.
2. Play a casual game in which you touch your pup's feet and reinforce with a treat, touch his belly and treat, and touch his collar and treat.
3. Play this game for several days with your youngster.

Phase Two

When your pup is very relaxed with this, you can make it a bit more challenging.

1. Instead of just touching your pup's foot, start to hold it lightly.
2. Treat your pup while you have the foot in hand.
3. Then start to play with your pup's toes. This is an important step to training your pup to accept nail trimming.

4. Next, tug lightly on your pup's collar and treat. Continue to tickle all the other parts of his body. Find those spots he loves best.

Phase Three

Now recruit your friends. It is important that pups learn to accept touching from a variety of people. Have them hold your pup and wiggle his toes and rub his chest. This will make trips into the world safe and pleasurable for your young pal.

Possible Challenges

Most dogs do not like a hand that comes right toward the top of their head. This is a natural reaction, and they will sometimes duck away. Turning your hand palm up and approaching

Trainer Talk

Puppies come in a variety of personalities. There are assertive pups, excitable pups, insecure puppies, confident puppies, dependent puppies, independent puppies, and sensitive puppies. These personalities are often observable by eight weeks. My Sheltie Scout was a very independent puppy who was not much interested in snuggling. Guess what kind of adult she is? Each type of pup requires a slightly different approach from you.

Puppies should learn to accept handling all over their body.

the pup's head from underneath easily solves this issue. All of the Canine Companions puppy raisers learn to instruct people who have asked permission to pet to reach for the chest rather than the head.

Most pups relish this game and come to love the feel of a person's hands. If your pup is fearful of being touched or growls at you at any time, seek the help of an experienced trainer or dog behaviorist.

Exercise #5: Back-and-Forth Recall

Goal: Teach your pup that coming to you is highly rewarding.
Ideal Age to Start: 8 weeks
Groundwork: None
Clicker: No

Background

In dog training, any exercise in which the pup is asked to come to you is called a "recall." There are a few *recall* games scattered throughout this book. Why a few? There is nothing more frustrating than a dog who won't come to you when you beckon. In addition, a good *recall* can be a matter of life and death. Imagine that your pup slips out the front door and is headed toward a busy street or jumps out of the car in a busy parking lot. Calling him to you could spell the difference between tragedy and a happy ending.

Pups are usually pretty good about coming for the first few weeks. You are the center of their universe. Then overnight something clicks and the pup realizes that he has choices. You can almost see the wheels turning: *Hmmm. This plant sure smells good. Is it worth it to stop sniffing and run to that person?* Your challenge as a trainer is to teach your pup that choosing you—the ultimate prize—will provide a bigger payoff than whatever else he's interested in. This process takes ongoing training over many months because the world is Disneyland for pups. If your pup looks at you and thinks *dull person*, you are in trouble.

I noticed an interesting phenomenon. Most puppy raisers understand that they must actively teach their pups to sit or lie down. But they think that the pup should come automatically. HA. Not only do pups have to be taught to come, but it takes much longer to teach a truly reliable *recall* than most other commands. With my pups, I work on the *recall* a bit every day for at least a year. Then I continue to maintain it for the dogs' whole lives by intermittently surprising them with a treat after they thunder in from the yard when I call. This is simply money in the bank.

The following game is a perfect first step. It also allows you to get eager-to-help children and friends involved.

Process

Phase One

This is a two-person game, so find a partner to play with you and your pup. Each of you should fill your pocket with small pieces of a healthy puppy treat. The pup should be on a 6-foot (2-m) leash.

1. Sit on the floor 6 feet (2 m) apart, facing your partner. The person who has the leash should give the pup a tiny treat.
2. Then toss the leash to your partner. This keeps the pup from wandering away.
3. Your partner should then call

In dog training, any exercise in which the pup is asked to come to you is called a "recall."

the puppy with a happy voice saying something such as "Puppy, puppy."

4. Keep your treats in your pocket or your training bag so that the pup gets them as reinforcement after he reaches you, not as a bribe. If you let the pup see the cookie first, he will learn to come only if he sees the treat.

5. As soon as the pup devours a treat given by your partner, she should toss the leash back to you. This keeps the pup from getting distracted and wandering off.

6. Immediately call the pup and treat him as soon as he arrives. Petting and lavish praise is nice too.

7. Repeat several times, taking turns with your partner. Stop before your pup tires of the game. Puppies have a very short attention span.

Play several times each day with your baby. As he gets into the game, put a long line on him so that you can sit farther apart. The only limit is how far you can toss the line accurately to each other. With the long line, there are occasional tangles, but it is worth the effort to make sure that your pup doesn't wander off.

Phase Two

This part of the game teaches the pup to come quickly and directly rather than just wander back and forth. Continue to sit on the floor facing your partner. Remove the pup's leash but leave the collar on.

Once your dog comes reliably on a long line, you can transition to reinforcing the command without one.

Trainer Talk

Informal training is often as powerful as formal lessons. In the case of the *recall*, I recommend that you keep small bowls of dog treats all around your house. I use a dry cereal because it holds up well over time. I call my pup dozens of times a day when I can tell he will come, which means that he is not sniffing, playing with a toy, or simply too far away. When he comes, I reinforce generously with treats. This goes on until the pup is at least a year old. He learns from week one that coming to me is a fun, rewarding game and he should be listening for me to beckon. I am very careful never to call if there is any chance my pup won't come, and I never call him for something he might not like, such as an ear cleaning.

1. Start by holding your pup's collar. Have your partner call him with food in her hand, using an enthusiastic, happy voice.
2. Let the pup strain slightly toward her, then release him.
3. After the pup races to her and gets the treat, she should put her hand in the pup's collar, then reverse the game with you calling and your partner restraining the pup just until he is primed to race to you. Remember to greet him happily and reinforce with food. You should play this both inside and outside.
4. Start using your command *come* as your pup is racing toward you. Gradually move the command to just before your partner releases the pup, when you can tell that he is coming to you for sure.

Phase Three

Once your pup runs back and forth with enthusiasm, it's time to play without the leash or holding the collar. This gives the pup more responsibility.

1. Start in a long hallway. This keeps the pup on the straight and narrow. A room or the yard offer too many distractions. You and your partner should sit at opposite ends of the hall.
2. With your treats at hand, call the pup back and forth. Remember to reward lavishly.
3. Once your pup is reliable, move this game to a room and then outside to a fenced area.

Possible Challenges

The delight of this game is that little can go wrong, because you don't ask too much too fast.

Real-Life Pups

At seven-and-a-half weeks, Jade loved the back-and-forth *recall*. Because she was getting most of her meals by hand, this game provided an easy way for her to earn food. Lauri and her partners called Jade by saying, "Pup pup" initially. After play for a few weeks, they began using her name while offering her treats. This helped her associate her name with something very positive.

If the pup is slow to come, simply reel him in very gently when he is on lead. Give lots of treats when he gets to you. If at any time the pup gets distracted, go back to the step before.

Be careful that you don't start calling your pup around the house. If he chooses not to come, you are teaching the opposite of what you want. Just go and gently get him if you want him, until he firmly understands what your calling means.

Exercise #6: Lap and Off

Goal: Teach your pup to lie comfortably across your lap while you pet, brush, or just visit, and to get off when asked.

Ideal Age to Start: 7 months

Groundwork: Your pup should be able to sit on command because that is the starting position for this game.

Clicker: Yes

Teaching your puppy the *lap* command is useful because it makes it easier to groom him and bond with him.

Trainer Talk

In puppy training, "discrimination" is a good word. It means that the pup is learning to discriminate between two similar behaviors or between times that it is okay to do something and times that it isn't. Learning not to jump on you in general and learning to perform the command *lap* when asked is one of your pup's first discriminations. Pups are capable of discriminating between many behaviors if you work with them on understanding the difference.

Background

Lap is a command commonly taught to future assistance dogs because it allows an owner with limited mobility to put on the cape that assistance dogs wear to identify themselves, to clean their pup's ears, or to brush him. It is a lovely command for pet puppies too, with many practical applications. It allows you to groom your pup without hunching over. It allows you to position your pup near someone who could not otherwise reach him for a pet. It provides a great opportunity to simply hold your adolescent pup and tell him how much you enjoy him. Big puppies will learn to drape across your lap while you are sitting in a chair. Toy dogs can perform *lap* if you sit on a pillow on the floor rather than on a chair.

If you are sitting in a chair to teach this command, choose one with no arms because it allows the pup to approach from your side.

For many pups, this game requires a bit of help the first time or two. Recruit a friend or family member to stand by in case the pup needs assistance.

As with all other commands, it is up to you to decide when this game starts and when it is over. If your pup starts to volunteer to get in your lap when you have not asked, don't reward him by petting. Just get up to go do something else.

Process

Phase One
1. Sit comfortably on your chair or pillow.
2. Use a treat to lure your pup into facing your leg at a right angle.
3. Have him sit. Later this will keep him from leaping into your lap before you are prepared.
4. Put your treat in your hand on the far side of your lap. Pat your lap with the hand closest to your pup. If he puts his paws up, use the treat to lure him clear across until he drapes comfortably across your thighs.
5. Repeat this game until your pup will drape across your lap in pursuit of the cookie. Generally, pups who are slow to believe this game is okay will get into it after two or three practice sessions.

If your pup hesitates or looks suspicious (*Hey, you can't fool me into putting my feet on you*), it is probably because you have worked with him on not jumping. You will need to show him that it is okay to get into your lap when you ask. Have your friend gently lift him from just behind the elbows and drape him across your lap. Once he is in position, click and treat, treat, treat.

When you are ready to get him off, gently push him off the same direction he came up. Some dogs just want to slip off the front of your legs, but it looks messy. Okay, call me picky.

Phase Two

1. Play the same game, but start using your *lap* command right after your dog gets comfortably draped.
2. After practicing at least 30 times with the food lure, it's time to fade the cookie from your hand. Lure your pup once to show him the game you want to play.
3. Then repeat the game without food in your hand, but pat your far leg to show that you want him to come up. If he gets it right without the lure, click and jackpot generously while he holds the *lap* position. For a couple of practice sessions, alternate luring and patting your leg to cue him.
4. When you want your pup to slide off your lap, start using your *off* command just as his paws hit the floor. Click and reinforce your pup for getting off when his feet hit the ground.

Real-Life Pups

In these photos you can see how this pup learns this command. He sits very nicely so that he is facing his handler. The pup's body language is a bit tentative initially. He is a bit unsure if it is okay to get his paws up there. When he chooses to get into his handler's lap, the handler marks the behavior and treats the pup liberally from his bag. This reassures the pup. In the last photo, you see a pup who is highly enthusiastic about playing this game.

Phase Three

1. Start using your *lap* command as your pup is on the way up. Try to time it so that he is definitely coming up but still moving.
2. Drop your food lure altogether, but continue to pat your lap if necessary.
3. When he gets it right, click or mark and offer several treats from your far hand.
4. Start using your *off* command as he is sliding off your legs.

Phase Four

Your pup should love this game now. You can start to use your command before he initiates the behavior. Once he is consistent with the behavior, start to mark and reinforce randomly. You can gradually stop patting your lap.

Phase Five

Extend the time your pup can hold *lap* by feeding him tiny bits while he maintains the position. Work your way up to 30 seconds as your pup gains strength.

Possible Challenges

If you have a pup who has a serious jumping problem, you may want to wait on this game until he understands that his feet stay on the floor unless he is invited to do otherwise. Despite the occasional challenges of teaching your dog the boundaries of this game, it is well worth the effort.

Chapter 8
Everyday Behaviors

Exercise #7: Love My Crate

Goal: Teach your pup to relax in the crate during the day and sleep in the crate at night.
Ideal Age to Start: 8 weeks
Groundwork: None
Clicker: No

Background

I can't imagine training a pup without using a crate. It gives him a safe place to rest and relax with a favorite toy while you are distracted with human work. It allows you to monitor your pup's movements, which makes housetraining relatively easy. The crate is also great for teaching your pup self-control and keeping him out of trouble when you are out of the house. We will talk more about this in subsequent crate games.

Crates (also known as kennels) come in a variety of sizes, from Italian Greyhound tiny to Newfoundland huge. Select one that allows your pup to stand comfortably and turn around easily. Don't use an overly large crate for your pup, or he might be encouraged to pee in one corner and relax in another corner. Start with a smaller size and purchase another when your pup outgrows the first.

Because dogs are genetically programmed to live in caves, the crate comes to represent safety and security. When bedtime is imminent, my dogs tap their feet in front of their individual crates, eager to race in and get a final bedtime treat. Once they gulp a tiny cookie, they flop down and relax so thoroughly that I rarely hear them move during the night.

In addition, a crate that is firmly secured inside the car is by far the safest way for a dog to travel. A pup left loose in your auto is at terrific risk in case of an accident, even a relatively minor one.

During the first couple of nights, let your pup sleep in a folding exercise pen rather than the crate. Either fold the pen until it is close to the size of a crate, or make it a bit bigger and put the crate inside with the door open. Often, when given a choice,

Because dogs are genetically programmed to live in caves, the crate comes to represent safety and security.

pups will choose to snooze in the crate. Usually somewhere between the third and seventh nights, you will be able to use the crate only because your pup is comfortable with sleeping in it.

Process

Phase One

Begin teaching this game on the day your pup comes home.

1. Start with your pup on leash so that he can't wander off.
2. Show him a small cookie and toss it to the bacsk of the crate. This is easiest with a wire crate, but any crate will work as long as it is large enough for your pup to enter it easily. The cookie should go to the back of the crate. Make sure to use a high-powered treat that your pup will really want. Most pups will follow the treat into the crate.
3. When he has all four feet inside, praise him and toss in another treat.
4. As soon as he has finished his snack, lure him out of the crate by showing him another cookie. Give him the cookie as soon as he is out. You want to be the one deciding when he exits.
5. Repeat the same exercise over several sessions, encouraging your pup follow the tossed cookie into the crate.

If, during any session, your dog goes back to the crate after you have lured him out, praise and reward him with a jackpot of several treats. It is great that he is taking this initiative to do what you are asking.

Phase Two

As soon as your pup readily chases the treat into the crate, you can progress to this second phase. Although you are hand-feeding most of your pup's food during this first month, crate training is the one exception.

1. Put a small portion of one meal into a bowl.
2. With no fanfare, place the bowl well back into the crate and let your dog go in to eat it on his own. Leave the door open.
3. Stand by to let him come out as soon as he is done.

Phase Three

Continue to feed a bit of each meal in the crate.

1. When your pup runs in, shut the door for a few seconds.
2. Before he fusses, lure him out as before.

Gradually increase the time you close the door by increments of five seconds. If at any point he becomes anxious, shorten the time the door is closed.

Phase Four

1. When your pup is ready for a nap, gently put him in the crate. Leave the door open.
2. Watch for him to wake and take him outside immediately. You might find it best to carry him outside the first week.

Phase Five

Select a toy your pup really likes. Remember how you are controlling those resources? It might be a safe chew toy, like a hollow Nylabone with a bit of peanut butter smeared inside.

1. Lure him into the crate and give him his toy. Close the door and stay nearby.
2. Let him chew for a few minutes.
3. Release him from the crate before he fusses. If you wait until he whines and then let him out, you are teaching him to demand that he get out.

Gradually extend the time that he stays in to chew.

Phase Six

1. Get your pup nice and tired before bedtime, and lure him into his crate, ideally placed next to your bed.
2. Close the door and turn out the lights. You might set the alarm to get up and take him out to potty before he wakes and whines to go out. Healthy pups will generally not foul their "home." (Usually the need to take a pup out during the night ends in a week or two.)
3. As soon you as you wake in the morning, whisk your pup out of the crate and carry him outside so that he can potty. Praise, praise, praise him when he relieves himself.
4. Bring him back in and put him in his pen or back into the crate with a chew toy while you get dressed.

Use a safe chew or treat toy to lure your dog into his crate and keep him occupied in there.

Trainer Talk

Most of us like winning a jackpot. Pups are no different. Puppy trainers use the term "jackpotting" to refer to giving the pup a series of treats as a method of telling him that he did something particularly wonderful. Jackpot your pup when he gets a new game for the first time or when he does something that you have asked extraordinarily well. Rather than giving the pup a handful of treats, deliver tiny bits one at a time for at least 15 seconds.

Phase Seven

Very quickly, your pup will start running inside the crate on his own. When he does, toss his cookie in with him.

Possible Challenges

Most dogs learn to love the crate quickly, particularly if the treats are good, but occasionally a dog is hesitant to go in. If this happens, go slower. Take your pup into the area you keep the crate. If he looks at it, praise and treat. When he takes a step toward it, praise him and place a treat in the direction of the crate. Go slowly. End each lesson if he gets one step closer. If he finally steps inside, throw a treat party. Resist the urge to simply push your pup into the kennel, because this will lower his trust in you.

At the same time that you are making a yellow brick road of treats to the crate, you can begin to feed your pup a small meal near the crate but not so close as to make him fearful. Each day move the bowl closer and then barely into the crate. As the pup becomes comfortable, move the bowl toward the back. Make sure not to close the door to trap the anxious pup. Taken slowly, he will find the crate a safe and reassuring place.

Occasionally, a pup may throw a gigantic tantrum when put in the crate at night. This is more common with adult dogs who have not been crated before, but an occasional pup will also demand his freedom, even if he has been slowly and carefully introduced to the crate. You don't want to reinforce this behavior by letting him out. If he barks and demands his release, let the neighbors know that you are not torturing him. You might try covering the crate with a blanket, leaving space for air circulation. Often when the visual stimulation is removed, the pup will start to relax. Covered or not, the pup will eventually get tired and go to sleep. Usually a pup prone to this protest repeats this behavior two more nights, each time with less enthusiasm. By the fourth night, he'll have been so busy playing outside and learning from you that he'll be happy to totter in and fall asleep.

Exercise #8: Housetraining on Steroids

Goal: Teach your pup to potty outside consistently.
Ideal Age to Start: 8 weeks
Groundwork: Love My Crate (Exercise #7) and Frontload the Clicker (Exercise #2)

Clicker: Best with the clicker, but you can use your marker word too.

Background

Stating the obvious, your most important job while you raise your pup is housetraining. This process requires your attention virtually for months, although the first few weeks are the most important. Although few folks admit it, an amazing number of dogs never get fully housetrained. They keep the carpet cleaning industry healthy.

There are five secrets to housetraining:

A pup may occasionally throw a tantrum when crated, but don't reinforce the behavior by letting him out.

1. First, you must create a system so that your pup never makes a mistake. I will describe a positive process for doing this in a moment.

2. You must have a method to contain your pup while he is learning to go outside. Otherwise you are bound to get distracted and your pup will wander out of your sight, and that mistake we are trying to prevent will happen. You can use a crate, or you can alternate the use of a crate and exercise pen. I prefer to use both because they give the pup some variety.

3. This next point may sound harsh, but it is too important to ignore: You need to recognize that any time your pup makes a mistake, it is your fault. You gave your pup too much freedom and the opportunity to make a mistake.

4. Any time your pup makes a puddle in the house it creates a smell that no cleaner can remove, from a pup's perspective. Being a dog, he will naturally want to go in that spot again.

5. Interestingly, small dogs are harder to housetrain than big dogs. Toy dogs are notoriously challenging. You must be particularly vigilant to raise a tiny dog who goes outside consistently. I speak from personal experience, having had four Papillons.

Overall, it works much better to reward your dog for going outside than to yell at and punish him for mistakes. In fact, yelling at your dog if you catch him going inside creates only one thing: a sneaky pup. He will learn very quickly to pee inside behind the couch where there is no danger of all that hollering. Any ruckus you create around housetraining will damage your relationship with your pup.

One last thing: Don't quit working on housetraining until your pup is at least six months old. This is approximately when canines are able to control themselves physiologically. So many pups seem to get the drill about going outside within weeks. Their puppy raiser starts to take it for granted that the pup will ask to go out. Then the first piddle appears inside. Remember that you wouldn't expect a human infant to have control in three weeks. Don't expect that from your new pal. Whenever puppy raisers share that their pup is perfect about going outside in just a few weeks I cringe, knowing that they will most likely relax their system and the pup will forget the rules.

Process

Phase One

This is the intensive plan for housetraining that is set up to allow no mistakes. It may seem like a lot of work, but it is well worth the investment. Remember that any mistakes simply mean you have allowed too much freedom. Tighten your routine and supervision.

1. If you use an exercise pen, keep it fairly small so that the pup doesn't feel he can walk to the far end to piddle. Put a tarp down under the pen in case he makes a mistake. Replace it if he does because it will hold the smell.
2. Divide each hour into three sections. Set your timer to keep you on track. For the first ten minutes, take your pup out to play with you. If he eliminates, click while he is going and offer a treat. Do your best to wear him out by training and playing. Next you have two choices. You can bring him in and play with him in a restricted area of the house. The blocked-off kitchen or blocked-off family room is perfect. During this period, you need to watch him the whole time. Don't let him get behind a piece of furniture where he might potty. If you don't have time

Real-Life Pups

At eight weeks, Tex was a typical Canine Companions pup, sweet and floppy. Tex's puppy raiser created a system for Tex that defined a "no mistakes" plan. Here is how he describes it:

1. At eight weeks, keep puppy in a crate or a pen when indoors. Remove puppy from the crate or pen to carry him outside to toilet at an interval your pup can handle. This ranges from one to three hours.
2. When puppy toilets, give him lots of praise.
3. Give the puppy no chance to toilet in the wrong place and he won't.
4. I use many crates and keep one in the bedroom, under my desk, in the car, and at my girlfriend's place.
5. When I can supervise the pup closely, I let him romp in my house for a few minutes but only just after he toileted outside and only with close supervision.

It is important to note here that for this plan to work, pups must get plenty of exercise. Every time you take your pup out, give him a chance to relieve himself. Then play and play and work on a lesson until your pup is tired and ready to relax in his crate or pen.

If your puppy makes a housetraining mistake, don't scold him—simply clean up the mess and pay more attention to signals that he has to potty.

to supervise, tie your pup's leash to your belt and go about your business. Let him just come along while you do your chores. Fifteen to 20 minutes is long enough for a small pup. Now for the next half hour or so, put your pup in the crate or exercise pen with a nice chew toy and let him nap. Don't get him out if he whimpers, because this will teach him to make noise to get released. He will settle down and relax if you have worn him out well.

3. When the hour timer goes off, get your pup up if he is still sleeping. Take him out immediately. If he is small enough, you may want to carry him to prevent a mistake on the way to the door. Put him down where you want him to go. Most pups go immediately after a nap. When he is going, click and treat profusely. Now it is playtime again, and soon it will be naptime. If your pup wakes up before the hour is over, whisk him out before he whines.

4. Each time you feed your pup, three times a day, take him out immediately. Most pups go right after they eat.

5. As soon as possible, keep your pup in his crate overnight. Most pups need to go out once in the night. I recommend that you set the alarm, bite the bullet, and get up to take him out. Don't play or fuss over him now. This is all business. As soon as he is done, return him to his crate. The moment you wake up in the morning, get your pup outside. You will probably need to carry him. As usual, click and treat for success.

Put him in his crate or exercise pen while you get dressed so that he can't get into trouble. Give yourself a gold star for each day that your pup has no mistakes.

Phase Two
After a week, start extending the play, hangout, and nap periods during the day. For example, play for 15 minutes and keep your pup tethered to you for a half hour. Put him in his crate for 45 minutes or so. Don't relax your vigilance. This phase will go on until the pup is six months old. By six months, a pup can remain comfortably in the crate for up to four hours as long as he gets enough exercise when he is out and about.

Phase Three
Gradually give your pup a bit more freedom each week. For example, he may be loose in the kitchen while you prepare lunch if he has just relieved himself outside. From six months to a year, add more privileges as he earns them. If he backslides, immediately return to the level of supervision at which he was successful.

Just one caution: If you take your pup to go visiting at a friend's house, don't assume that he will be a good guest. Many pups who have seemed housetrained make a mistake in a new setting. Remember that dogs and puppies have trouble with generalization. While your pup is under a year old, supervise him carefully in every new setting. Take him outside and reward him generously when he goes in a new setting.

Possible Challenges
It is worth saying that housetraining can be more difficult with some dogs than others. As previously noted, toy breeds are famous for being challenging to housetrain. This may be partially

Trainer Talk
"Generalization" is a term that refers to the ability to take one piece of learning and apply it in a new setting. Pups and dogs do not generalize well. They will frequently learn a behavior at home and then at class or at a friend's house they will act as if they have never done it before. A common mantra in puppy class is: *But he does it at home!* It is the trainer's job to re-teach the pup every command in a variety of locations until it clicks for the dog that he can do the behavior everywhere. If you understand this, it will save you lots of frustration.

This concept is particularly important with housetraining. Pups often learn the routines at home and appear to understand that they need to go out to relieve themselves. But then in a new house, they squat on the carpet. They haven't generalized potty rules to every house. When you take your pup to any new place, assume that he does not know the rules and restrict his movement as you did when he was a pup. Reward like mad when he does go outside in the new setting.

because owners are less offended by the smaller quantities of waste and don't invest the necessary energy to housetrain. In addition, unaltered males can be particularly challenging because some have a strong drive to mark. *Hey, I was here!* They may be fine until another dog comes to visit and then the piddling wars begin. You can prevent this by paying special attention when you have doggy houseguests.

The other challenge with dog training is human. Monitoring a pup's every move until he is six months is hard work. As soon as a pup appears to understand that he is to go outside, puppy raisers naturally let down their guard. The pup is allowed to wander where he can't be seen, and the schedule breaks down. In puppy training classes I hear this sad story all the time despite exhortations not to relax. Once the pup goes inside, you need to go back to your old system and stick to it much longer.

Exercise #9: That's My Name

Goal: Teach your pup to look at you in acknowledgment when you say his name.
Ideal Age to Start: 8 weeks
Groundwork: Frontload the Clicker (Exercise #2)
Clicker: Yes

Background

Generally our pups learn their names despite us. We start calling our pup by his name from the moment we bring him home. We say his name when his breakfast is ready, when we want him to go outside, and when we want him to stop whining. We use his name to tell him that we love him. His name becomes part of the flood of words that he really doesn't understand or pay attention to. Gradually his name filters through, but it becomes something the pup only reacts to when he chooses.

In some cases, we actually teach the pup to ignore his name. We do this by saying it when we have little hope that the pup will respond. For example, what do you yell when your pup takes off after the cat? His name. What does he learn? Darn, that person is noisy.

It makes more sense to systematically teach your pup his name. This is fairly easy to do if you use your clicker and are a bit patient about using his name during his first weeks at home.

Process

Phase One

When you bring your pup home, don't use his name. Ask your family members to call him something generic, such as "puppy puppy." Use that as much as you want since you won't use it long term.

1. As soon as your pup is used to the clicker and knows that it means a treat will follow, put him on a leash so that he doesn't wander off.
2. Start this game by quietly saying only your dog's name when he is just sitting near

   you and not looking at you.

3. When he looks at you, immediately, click and treat. Then ignore him until he looks away.
4. Quietly say his name once. When he looks at you, you know what to do. Click and treat. Stay quiet otherwise so that he doesn't get flooded with words.
5. Repeat this game for several days until your pup is very consistently looking at you when you use that name.

Phase Two
Now start to work off lead.
1. Surprise your pup many times during the day by quietly saying his name. Make it spontaneous and fun.
2. As soon as he looks toward you, click and treat. Don't add extraneous cues or prompts such as "hurry up" or "come on." This is simply about responding to his name.
   Continue to use only your pup's real name during this game. Continue to use "puppy puppy" when you feel the need to chat at other times.

Phase Three
When you take your pup on his field trips (see Exercise #21: Meet the Goblins [Physical Objects]), start to play the name game.
1. When he is mildly distracted, say his name and then click and treat for a response. Make sure that the environment is not so stimulating that he won't be successful.
2. Gradually increase the challenge until your pup will respond to his name regardless of what is going on.
3. Begin to use your pup's name as a part of daily life. Continue to expect that when you use his name, he will check in. Occasionally click and treat to maintain the behavior.

Possible Challenges
I find that the biggest challenge for puppy raisers is not using the puppy's name as an ongoing mantra. When I inquire why they have just said, "Pookie, Pookie, Pookie," they inevitably reply that they are trying to get their dog's attention. Interestingly, they are teaching their dog to completely

ignore his name. Use this simple rule: Say your pup's name only once. If you say his name and get no response, you can assume that he does not understand or he has not been reinforced enough to care about responding. In that case, go back to playing the game as described.

Exercise #10: I Can Sit

Goal: Teach your dog to sit reliably and to remain seated.
Ideal Age to Start: 8 weeks
Groundwork: Put a buckle collar on your pup the day he arrives home. Also teach Frontload the Clicker (Exercise #2).
Clicker: Yes

Background

Teaching pups to sit is relatively easy because they sit all the time on their own. In this game, you are simply teaching your pup to plop his bottom down when you ask, no matter where he is or what is going on around him. You will also teach him to remain sitting for a period of time.

Surprise your pup many times during the day by quietly saying his name; this should be a spontaneous, fun lesson.

This exercise provides two specific opportunities for you as a trainer. First, you can practice using command words correctly. You will progress from using no command word at all to using the word to initiate the *sit* behavior. Second, it is the perfect exercise to practice your timing with the clicker. Your click should coincide with the exact moment your pup's bottom makes contact with the ground.

For some reason there is a tendency to hunch over and stare at our pups when we ask them to do something such as *sit*. This is a bad idea for two reasons: The posture is intimidating to dogs, and dogs are body language experts. If you hunch over consistently, your pup will believe that he can't sit unless you are looming over him. Unless you are bending over to lure your dog, stand up straight and relax your body.

Process

Phase One

1. Get your leash, your clicker, and a pocket of good treats. Snap the leash onto your pup. If it is his first time, he may be a bit startled to find that he can't wander

Trainer Talk

"Distraction" is a common word in trainer lingo. It refers to anything that might be more interesting to your pup than you. Big distractions are commonly other dogs and other people if your pup is very social. The goal of all training is to teach your pup to pay attention to you no matter what the distractions. For example, a well-trained dog can pay attention to you even with other dogs running nearby. However, this is a process that takes place over many months and takes great patience on your part. Any time your dog is unable to ignore the distractions, you have chosen a setting that is too stimulating for his level of development. Just train in a place that is a bit quieter for a while. Then add the distractions gradually.

wherever he wants. Just stand still and let him explore the limits of the leash. Most pups accept the leash remarkably quickly.

2. As soon as he relaxes, put a cookie on your open hand. With your palm up, show your pup the food near his nose.
3. Move the treat slowly to a spot above your pup's forehead. If you move it at the correct speed, he will lift his head to follow the food, and his bottom will automatically go down.
4. As soon as his rear hits the ground, click, pause a second or two, and deliver a treat. Keep your mouth quiet and let the clicker do your talking. If your pup is small, you may want to start this work on your knees, but after a few sessions, stand up.
5. Be patient. Don't talk or push on your pup. If your pup doesn't follow the treat, move it more slowly. Puppy eyes are not very good. If he backs up, just position him with his bottom to a wall or sofa.
6. Repeat this game 30 to 50 times over several teaching sessions. Remember not to ask your little baby to do too much in one session. Sitting three to five times in one lesson is plenty. Remember to stop training while the pup is still having fun.

Phase Two

Now it's time to transition to having your pup sit next to you rather than in front of you. This is the correct working position for a pup.

1. Gently position your pup next to a wall or any flat surface. Lure him into a *sit* as you have been doing, click, and reinforce. During this phase, you can start using your command word *after* your pup's bottom is on the ground. He will hear the word when he has already been successful. This will delay your click a moment.
2. Click after you say the command, pause, and deliver the cookie.
3. Repeat this game 30 to 50 times.

Phase Three

It's time to drop the use of the food lure now. Keep your food treats in your training bag.

1. Raise your hand as if you were still holding the treat. This is called a body cue. Your pup, who has been well conditioned by the motion, will sit.
2. Mark the moment his body hits the ground, using your clicker or marker word "yes," and reinforce generously.
3. Once your pup is responding consistently to the body cue, start using your command word *while* he is on the way to sitting.
4. Remember to do the same number of repetitions as you did previously.

Phase Four

Now you are going to drop the body cue and use your verbal command only.

1. Give your *sit* command *before* your pup has initiated the behavior. When he plops down, click and deliver a jackpot the first and second time. Then repeat 30 to 50 times with just one treat.
2. There is a natural tendency, once we start using a command word to initiate a behavior, to start saying, "Pookie, *sit*, *sit*, *sit*." This effectively teaches the pup that you didn't mean it the first time. Say the pup's name and the command word just once. If you have laid the foundation as described, he will sit.

   Practice the *sit* daily with your pup. Continue working him at least half the time against a variety of walls so that he is comfortable working next to you.

Phase Five

Next you are ready to teach your pup to stay seated. Learning to sit and learning to stay seated are two completely different parts of a pup's learning. This distinction comes up all the time in puppy classes: *My puppy sits but he keeps getting up.* Yup. Pups need to be taught to stay seated using as methodical a plan as you have implemented with the command itself.

1. To teach duration, the performance of a command over time, have your pup sit.
2. Then feed him a series of tiny treats while he remains seated. If your pup is lively and wants to pop up, you will need

The *sit* command teaches your pup to plop his bottom down when you ask, no matter where he is or what is going on around him.

to feed quickly. If your pup is quiet, you will be able to feed at a slower pace. Your goal is to reward your pup at a speed that makes it worth his while to stay seated.

3. Initially, have him stay seated just a couple of seconds and then release him to stand up by lightly tickling his chest. Over the next couple of months of training, space the treats out so that your pup can sit up to a minute before he gets a cookie.

Phase Six

1. Ask your pup to sit in increasingly distracting settings.
2. Continue to click each successful performance. If your pup can't comply in a stimulating environment, back off to somewhere he can be successful and gradually increase the challenge.

Phase Seven

Now that your pup is comfortable with sitting when asked, you want to wean him from continuous cookies. It is tempting to quit reinforcing your pup with cookies the minute he sits nicely, but most puppy raisers do this prematurely. Remember that any behavior will disappear if it is not reinforced. No paycheck for a couple of months and I bet you quit going to work.

Through Phase Four, reinforce 100 percent of the times that your pup sits. Then you can start to reinforce less often. This means that you click and treat for some *sits* but not for others. Remember, you can improve your pup's performance by reinforcing those *sits* you like the best, such as the straightest ones. Communicate that you like straight *sits* the best and you will, of course, see more of that behavior. Be careful not to set your criteria so high that your pup can't be successful.

You can also just reinforce intermittently. Simply decide that you will click and reinforce three *sits* and then skip the fourth, or reinforce every other *sit*. Remember not to click the ones you don't plan to feed since you must give a cookie when you have used the clicker. If I'm not going to give my pup a treat, I just say something such as "Good job" so that he knows I've noticed his effort.

Your dog should learn to sit in increasingly distracting settings.

Possible Challenges

Remember that the clicker is only as powerful as your timing with the click. If you have your pup sit but then you click as he stands up, you have reinforced the second behavior rather than the one you wanted. The good news is that pups are very resilient, so forgive yourself if you make an occasional mistake. It is better to click at odd times now and then than to give up on the clicker.

Another possible challenge is that your pup will want to sit where he can see your face. If you have a pup who keeps maneuvering to look at you, simply do extra work using a wall or barrier as I described. If he gets adequate reinforcement for sitting next to you, he will choose that behavior.

Exercise #11: Nip Those Nails

Goal: Work with your pup to accept nail trimming.
Ideal Age to Start: 8 weeks
Groundwork: Topnotch puppy breeders condition pups to accept nail trimming from the time they are just a few weeks old. If you are purchasing from a breeder, ask what method she has used.
Clicker: No

Background

Puppy nails grow just like ours do. Left to grow without regular trimming, they can literally cripple a dog.

You have two options for nail trimming tools: Choose either traditional clippers available at any pet store (I use a cat-sized clipper for my toy dogs and the regular size for larger dogs) or a newer option, a small grinder called a Dremel. These are available at hardware stores and larger variety stores. The battery-powered Dremel with a

Trainer Talk

One thing that puppy raisers often underestimate is how many times one must reinforce the pup for a desired behavior before he really knows what you want. It is safe to think of at least 120 repetitions of any behavior with reinforcement before your dog understands the correct behavior. Of course, this varies with individual dogs and breeds. Generally the more your pup learns, the fewer the repetitions needed for him to learn the next thing. This may seem like a lot of practice, but it is no different than with kids. As a teacher, I was often told that students needed to hear things 300 times before they internalized them. This makes pups seem seriously gifted.

Once your pup consistently performs a command in a variety of settings, you can practice it less frequently. If your pup plays a familiar game once or twice a week, he will remember it well.

sandpaper sleeve is my tool of choice because it is easy to maneuver and control. There are also Dremels that plug in, but I don't recommend these. This type rotates so quickly that it is easy to grind off more nail than you planned.

Nail trimming should be on your calendar like clockwork, ideally taking place once a week to keep the nails short. Once a month is the longest you should ever go. The other benefit of trimming this often is that your pup gets used to the routine. When weeks go by between trimmings, the pups tend to see the process as something scary.

Trim your dog's nails once a week to keep tham at a comfortably short length.

Few dogs take nail trimming in stride. This makes it doubly important to teach your pup to accept this process while he is small and manageable. Grooming shops are filled with dogs who find nail trimming terrifying. This is simply not necessary if you start early and trim regularly, following the plan below.

Before we start, here is an important bit of information on nail anatomy. Puppy nails have a blood vessel inside. This blood supply is called the quick. You can see the quick if you have a pup with white nails. Unfortunately, it is not visible in black nails. If left untrimmed, the quick goes to the end of the nail. This creates a bad cycle because it is difficult to trim the nail without nicking the quick. On the other hand, if you trim regularly, the quick

retreats back up the nail. If you allow the quick to get to the end of the nail, you will need to clip or grind a bit off every few days so that the vessel recedes. If you do ever nick the quick, it is not the end of the world, although your pup may act like it is for a moment. Just apply a bit of dry cornstarch and the slight bleeding will stop.

If you are uncomfortable with nail trimming, take your pup to a gentle friend or dog groomer. This is a good time to ask for help.

Process

Phase One
During your pup's first few days at home, handle his toes regularly. Hold his paws gently. You can make this a separate game or combine it with cradling.

Phase Two
After just two or three days, bring out the clippers or Dremel. Your goal is to get your pup familiar with your tool of choice. This phase should take just two or three days.

1. If you plan to use the clippers, hold your pup in your lap and softly tap the clippers on all sides of his front and back nails. If he shows any anxiety, tap gently and then offer a treat. Tap again and offer a treat. Do this for a couple of days. Don't clip anything.
2. If you have decided to use the Dremel, turn it on and hold it in your hand farthest from the pup while you sit on the floor and feed him. This gets him used to the sound.
3. During each meal bring the tool a bit closer until it is within 1 foot (.3 m) of the pup. If he is anxious at all, move it away and then inch it closer as he relaxes.
4. Next, hold your pup in your lap. Hold him with one arm and The Dremel in the other. Turn on the tool and touch your pup's foot quickly with the handle so that he feels the vibration.
5. Very gradually, extend the time you touch him up to approximately five seconds. Feel free to treat him to make the experience rewarding. Don't grind anything at this point.

Phase Three
Most folks prefer to clip or grind with a small or medium-sized pup on a stable table because it discourages the dog from darting off. It should be low enough that you can drape your arm over the pup. With our smallish dogs, I use our kitchen table with a towel to cover it. This may be impractical with giant breeds, but you can trim your dog's nails on the floor.

Real-Life Pups
Scout the Sheltie gave me fits when I tried to trim her nails, although I had plenty of experience. Rather than fighting, I found a local groomer who was so confident that Scout relaxed. After a few months, Scout knew that trimming was something she had to put up with, and even though she doesn't love it, she accepts it.

Trainer Talk

An important goal in training is to prevent power struggles that your pup wins. Nail trimming is obviously one of those situations. If your pup struggles, don't give up and put him down because the message to him is that resisting pays. Hang on and do at least one more nail before you end the game. Then consider getting someone experienced to help, as I did with Scout.

   This rule has other applications. For example, if you pick your pup up and he struggles or growls, never put him down right away. What would the message be? Better to hold him gently until he relaxes. Give him several treats when he relaxes and then set him down on your terms.

1. Practice putting your pup on the table, using plenty of treats. Make sure that he has a collar on so that you can hold him safely.
2. When he relaxes, drape your arm over his back and touch the clippers or Dremel to his foot with your other hand as you have been doing. If he accepts the process, give him a cookie and repeat. Practice with him facing both directions.
3. Next, start lifting his leg from the elbow using the arm over his back. You will trim or grind while holding that leg.

Phase Four
It's time to clip or grind. Make sure that you have a pile of good treats available.
1. Put your pup up on the table.
2. Drape your arm over him and lift his leg from the elbow. Either clip or grind one nail.
3. Give him a treat.
4. Trim the next nail. Treat.

Possible Challenges
Some pups inherently dislike nail trimming despite the puppy raiser's best efforts. For pups like this, the best approach is to clip or Dremel one nail only, reinforce the pup with a cookie, and call it a day. Then do another nail the next day. The short interaction keeps the pup from winding himself into a frenzy. If this doesn't work after a couple of weeks, take your pup to a relaxed professional to get the chore done regularly.

Exercise #12: Home Alone
Goal: Teach your pup that he is okay by himself for a reasonable period of time.
Ideal Age to Start: 9 weeks
Groundwork: The pup should have some experience resting in the crate or exercise pen with you in the vicinity.
Clicker: No

Background

As I wrote in Chapter 2, dogs are highly social beings. This is because they descend from animals that survived in packs. From a canine's perspective, being alone is unnatural.

Many dogs are surrendered to rescue organizations each year because they freak out when left alone. Dogs who are anxious often damage things as a way of calming themselves.

It is up to you to teach your pup that he is safe by himself so that he can relax. This is best done through a sequential process so that your pup learns that you will return and he is okay when you are not visible. The process requires that you use either a crate or exercise pen to keep him out of mischief.

Some puppy raisers often create separation problems by keeping young pups with them 24/7 past the first week. This is frequently true with folks who have retired or work at home. After all, the pup is so darling. Remember that a significant part of your training effort is to prepare the pup for everything that he will need to understand when he is grown. Unless you never go out the rest of your life, being alone is one of those things. Even if you need to create an artificial situation to leave, do it. Try heading out for a latte each day.

Your pup should learn how to spend relaxing time alone.

Real-Life Pups

On Jade's first day at home, Lauri had to leave her to go teach agility classes on the field just beyond the house. Each class was about an hour long. There was no time to get Jade used to staying alone. Lauri left her contained in her exercise pen with a chew toy since she initially disliked the crate. Lauri locked her other dogs in another room so there wouldn't be any inappropriate interactions. When she went outside, Lauri could hear Jade barking non-stop.

When there was a break between classes, Lauri let Jade out for exercise and a potty break. Jade was ecstatic until she went back in her pen. As soon as Lauri left, the barking began. There was simply nothing Lauri could do about this since she knew if she brought the pup to the field Jade would never learn to amuse herself on her own. Since Lauri has no close neighbors, she let her bark. The second day Jade was hoarse, but she still gave barking her best effort. The third day she barked a bit, but it was half-hearted. The fourth day there was barely a peep. When Lauri would go in to walk her, she was either chewing on her toy or napping. The problem never reared its head again. If your pup does some barking initially and you don't live in the country, you might want to let your neighbors know what is going on and that you have a plan to teach your pup to be quiet.

Process

Phase One
1. Put your pup in his exercise pen or crate for a moment or two several times each day. It is best after some exercise so that he is ready to nap. Give him a special toy that is safe for him to have when you are not supervising.
2. Come and go from the room where he is situated. Go out of his sight. If he fusses, don't comfort him or chastise him. Just ignore him until he is quiet for a bit.
3. Then let him out of his crate or pen and head to the yard because he will likely need to potty. Resist the urge to fuss over him when you let him out.

Phase Two
1. Leave the pup for a bit longer, and go into the garage or yard for a few minutes.
2. Come back and leave again. Remember to let the pup out only when he is quiet. If you let him out when he is fussing, he'll learn that fussing pays off.

Phase Three
1. When your pup takes the previous step in stride, it's time to hit the road.
2. Get your pup in his pen or crate, and give him his special toy.
3. Get in your car and drive away. Stay away just a few minutes—a drive around the block is fine.
4. Come in the house without making it a big deal.
5. Wait a couple of minutes and then let him out and take him outside. Hesitating a bit before

If you're not going to be home for more than four hours at a time, consider hiring a dog walker to give your pup some fresh air and exercise.

you take him out teaches him that there is no benefit to getting crazy when you arrive home.

Phase Four

Gradually extend the time you are away. The time shouldn't be longer than your pup can stay comfortable without going outside and never longer than four hours until he is at least six months old and able to control himself. Continue to be matter of fact when you come home so that your pup takes coming and going in stride.

If you need to be out of the house longer than four hours, I would recommend that you find a reliable pet sitter to stop in. When Scout was a baby, I was still working in education. I had to be gone many hours, so I hired a pet sitter to stop by midday and walk her.

Phase Five

It is fine to crate your dog every time you go out if you follow these guidelines. If he has a busy life, he will always appreciate a good rest in his "den." On the other hand, you might decide that at a certain age you would like to try leaving him out. At about a year, I decide whether to keep a pup crated or start leaving him loose with the other dogs.

If I opt to leave the pup out, I make my first trips short and then stretch them out as the pup proves himself reliable. When I begin leaving him loose, I pick up all tempting chew toys, such as the television remote and the trash baskets, to give him the greatest chance of success. If at any time your pup becomes destructive, go back to crating when you leave.

Possible Challenges

There are rarely any challenges with pups introduced to time alone in this way. Most problems are the result of pups being tossed out in the yard or locked up in the house for too many hours. Once a dog has a full-blown case of separation anxiety, you definitely need to crate train him so that he has a safe place to stay when you need to leave. Then you must follow the same process of leaving him for very short periods and gradually extending them.

Remember that a pup or dog should never be punished for destruction done while you are away. It is our fault if we don't help them feel safe while we are gone. Punishment will simply convince your dog that you are scary and will do nothing to address the anxiety of having you leave.

Exercise #13: Getting Dressed

Goal: Introduce your pup to the training equipment you plan to use.

Ideal Age to Start: 9 weeks

Groundwork: Your first step is to decide which type of equipment you plan to use on your pup during training sessions. As you read earlier, I strongly recommend either the head halter or a no-pull harness. For the majority of dogs, I hope you will try the head halter. It gives you the most control over your pup without any need for corrections. However, it will not work on dogs with a

Trainer Talk

Pups are much happier alone when they have a toy to pass the time. But not all puppy toys are created equal. In fact, some are quite dangerous because a big piece can cause choking or lodge in the pup's digestive tract. The best toys for those times when you are not present are nearly indestructible and nonconsumable. When you select your pup's toys, consider the following:

- one-piece bone-like toys, such as Nylabones, which are available in many different flavors and sizes
- rubber stuffable-type toys with a hole you can coat with a bit of peanut butter or stuff with biscuits that are nearly impossible to extract
- sterilized natural bones that you can also stuff with peanut butter or a bit of cheese

You may like a certain toy, but your pup must also value it. Once you know what your pup loves to gnaw on, save that special toy for the times you leave him crated.

short muzzle or on dogs who are particularly sensitive to pressure on the face. The no-pull harness is a good alternative for these dogs. Naturally, if one tool doesn't work, it is okay to regroup and try another.
Clicker: No

Background

When you purchase either the head halter or harness, check the sizes carefully. When I purchased my first harness, the store staff helped me fit and adjust it. Don't be shy about asking for assistance. Make sure that you ask someone to demonstrate how to put the head halter on, because this has baffled many smart folks.

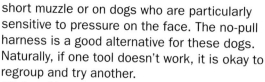

Real-Life Pups

Canine Companions pups are introduced to the head halter at eight weeks. By ten weeks, most pups are comfortable wearing it during an entire training class.

Most pups will go through two or three sizes of either head halter or harness as they mature. Make sure to watch for either piece of equipment becoming too tight, and replace it right away.

Once you purchase your training device, your next step is to get your pup comfortable with wearing it. The earlier your pup starts wearing the head halter or harness, the better he will accept it as part of life. Best of all, you can start using it in your training sessions right away.

Both the harness and head halter require that you introduce them systematically to your pup. The brochures for no-pull harnesses include an excellent description of the introductory process. They suggest that you start by attaching the leash to both collar and harness, which keeps the harness from twisting. Next they instruct you to practice standing and then walking next to the pup while gently pulling straight up to help him understand the new pressure on his body. Once he is comfortable, you can start teaching your pup while he is wearing his harness.

The head halter requires a more extensive introduction because the band around the nose looks and feels different than anything the pup has experienced. The Canine Companions puppy raisers use the sequential process described below to introduce assistance dog pups to the halter. I have observed that the earlier a pup is introduced to the head halter, the greater the chance of success. If you wait until six months to put a head halter on your dog, you're likely to have a bigger challenge on your hands. If you adopt an older pup, you should still work with the head halter, but take your time with the steps described. It is certainly worth the investment if you can get your pup to accept it.

One last note: Your pup should never play with other pups in a harness or head halter. He can certainly wear them to kindergarten class, but always remove them before playtime so that the other pups can't grab them.

Process

Phase One

1. Fill your pocket with cookies that your pup values.
2. Pull the noseband up through the ring.
3. Slip the noseband onto your pup's muzzle.
4. Give a treat and take it off. Don't even think about fastening anything. Just slip it on and off and treat each time. Repeat this for a couple of days and as many times as you can stand. If your pup is squirmy, do it while a partner holds the pup.

Phase Two

1. This time, slip on the noseband.
2. Grasp the two pieces that will fasten behind your pup's head and hold them in the correct position. Don't snap them.
3. While you hold the head halter on, treat and praise your pup.
4. Repeat a number of times over a couple of days.

Phase Three

1. At mealtime, when you are ready to hand-feed your pup his meal, slip on the head halter and snap it closed at the back of his head.
2. Immediately start feeding him before he has time to react.
3. As soon as he is done eating, take it off. Make sure that he doesn't run off and try to remove it.
4. Repeat for at least two days.

Phase Four

Now you are going to take your pup on a walk while he wears the head halter. This step is very important because it allows him to feel the head halter while he walks without feeling a great deal of pressure from it.

1. Slip on the head halter, snap the leash onto his flat collar, and start walking right away.
2. Praise and treat your pup generously if he ignores the halter and walks with you.
3. Repeat this game for two or three days or until your pup walks along with you and ignores it.

Whether you purchase a head halter or a harness, ask store staff how to fit it properly.

Trainer Talk

Earlier I mentioned that reinforcement cookies for training have different values, depending on how your pup views them. A high-value treat is whatever really lights him up. In our house, hotdog bits or a bit of chicken meat fall into this category. A low-value treat is something that the pup enjoys but doesn't get crazy over. A bit of dry food may be high or low value, depending on the pup. I recommend a high-value treat for introducing the head halter to your dog because it is completely different from anything he has felt before. Low-value treats are generally adequate for introducing the harness, which usually surprises the pup less.

Phase Five
1. Snap your leash onto the head halter and take off for a short walk. Leave your leash loose. Let the pup explore the consequences of pulling on the halter.
2. Reward your pup frequently for walking along nicely with you.
3. Take the halter off before the pup starts to worry about it.
4. Gradually extend your walks each day until you can travel down a short block. Now your pup is ready to train in the halter.

For several months, continue to provide a high-value treat to your pup each time you put his head halter on so that he develops a positive association.

Possible Challenges

Most pups do just fine during the first four phases unless the puppy raiser makes the mistake of letting the dog remove the head halter on his own. Once the pup does this, he'll get it in his head that he can remove it and will keep trying. Do your best to never let this happen.

At the fifth phase, the pup starts to feel the pressure of the head halter. Some pups will try to rub the halter off on your leg or the ground. If your pup does this, gently pull him up by his flat collar and get walking so that he thinks about other things. Most pups outgrow this effort in a few days, as long as they are not successful at rubbing it off.

Occasionally, even given the best of introductions, a pup will simply not relax with a head halter on. My Sheltie Scout wore the head halter, but she was so miserable that I eventually opted to switch to a harness with her. I have since discovered that she is particularly sensitive to touch all over her body. While I don't recommend giving up easily on this useful device, you must balance its use with keeping your dog excited about working with you.

Exercise #14: Casual Heel

Goal: Teach your dog to walk next to you on a loose leash.
Ideal Age to Start: 10 weeks
Groundwork: Your pup can start this exercise on a buckle collar and leash but should transition to the head halter or no-pull harness as soon as he is comfortable working in one of those.
Clicker: No; use your marker word in place of the clicker.

Background

I am always amazed by how many people I see walking down the street with their dogs dragging them at the end of the leash like a sled dog. Big-dog owners often look as if they are about to become airborne.

These owners have missed a great opportunity to teach their dogs the self-control needed to walk nicely next to them on a loose leash. Every dog can learn to walk nicely on the leash, even during unexpected distractions. There are several clear benefits to teaching your dog the casual *heel*:

- Walking next to you is actually better exercise for your dog than pulling on the leash because the dog has to demonstrate self-control, which takes a good bit of effort.
- Walking next to you builds your relationship. Dogs who haul on ahead of you have no interest in what you are doing.
- It is fun to have your dog walk with you. It is not fun to be just an anchor on your dog's walk.

This training exercise is called a casual *heel* because it does not require your dog to be as exacting as in the obedience ring. Competitive obedience dogs must stay glued to their handler's side and stare up at the handler's face. Unless you are headed toward serious competition, it is enough to expect your pup to walk close to your side on a loose lead rather than walking along with his attention on everything but you.

The approach I am going to teach you is based on rewarding your pup for walking next to you. Gradually the pup learns that the *heel* position—his right ear next to your left knee—is the most rewarding place to be. The approach that I will describe has worked for literally hundreds of assistance puppies in training and a wide variety of future agility dogs.

While many of the games in this book take very little time, the casual *heel* requires you to work

The casual *heel* teaches your dog to walk by your side on a loose leash.

with your dog over several months to achieve perfection—that is, he will stay right next to you even when something very exciting happens, such as another dog approaching. I cannot think of a better use of your training time.

The challenge in teaching a dog to walk next to you is that he has to enjoy being next to you more than he enjoys sniffing, pulling, or charging after cats. As with teaching your dog to come to you when called, your goal is to be more interesting than an exciting world of smells and sights. Your power lies in your ability to deliver high-powered, high-value treats. Remember when we talked about the importance of controlling your pup's resources? This is another opportunity to use them to reinforce, reinforce, and reinforce the behavior you want.

I have noticed in working with newer trainers that they sometimes restrain their pup by their side and mistake that for heeling. If your leash is taut, you are holding your pup back rather than teaching him to walk there on his own. Restraining a pup never teaches him self-control.

When you are training your pup for the casual *heel*, you should strive for what trainers call a "J-leash." That is, your leash hangs straight down and then has a short loop back up to the pup's collar. The J-leash shows that the pup is working rather than being held captive.

You may notice that in this exercise, I don't mention the clicker. I've found over the years that the clicker is just one too many things to manage when teaching the casual *heel*. You can substitute your marker word "yes!" when you want to let your pup know that he is doing a fine job by choosing to walk by your side.

It is important to remember that dogs do not understand mixed messages. In this case, your pup will get a mixed message if you ask him to walk next to you sometimes and then let him pull you other times. I notice that puppy raisers often let their little ones drag them from the car into the classroom and then expect them to heel during class. This is very confusing to a pup. They simply cannot understand that it is okay to pull one minute but

If you're walking recreationally with your dog, such as on a hike, use a different leash so that he can differentiate between fun time and training time.

Real-Life Pups

In this series of photos, you'll see a Canine Companions pup in the three phases of learning to heel: following the lure (left), following a lure that is not above his head (center), and heeling without a lure but getting rewarded regularly from the magic training bag (right). Your pup can learn to do this too.

not the next. From the minute you leash your pup up for a lesson, he must always follow the same rules you've established. In this case, he should be thinking: *When my head halter is on, it's my job to walk right next to this leg.* When I say this in class, puppy raisers often panic. They ask whether their pup can ever just walk recreationally at the end of the leash, such as on a hike. The answer is yes—but only with the following guidelines:

- Put him on a different leash, such as an expandable leash, so that he knows he isn't going to work.
- Attach him to the flat collar instead of the head halter or harness, both of which tell him that he is going to work.
- Use your release word (see Exercise #18: Release) so that he knows it's appropriate for him to relax.
- Never let him pull you.

Process

Phase One

1. Start with your pup on leash at your left side.
2. Hold the leash across the front of your body in your right hand. In either case, your left hand must be free to deliver treats.
3. Load your left hand with small, soft treats. This hand is like a slot machine that pays off with a bit of food each time your pup chooses to walk next to you without pulling.
4. Hold your left hand next to your thigh with your palm back. If you are starting with a young

pup, there is a good chance that you will have to hunch over a bit to get the treat low enough for him to see it. When your pup sees the food, start walking so that he follows your hand. If by any chance he doesn't focus on the food, change treats.

5. As your dog walks next to you for just a few steps, use your marker word and treat. Your goal is to get him to choose to walk right next to you because it is a rewarding place, so you do not want to drag him. If he gets distracted, talk sweetly to him but resist using his name over and over or he will soon learn to ignore it.

6. Each time you mark the correct behavior, dole out a small bit of food. Many pups need to stop to eat. Try to reward your dog when he is in the correct position with his ear next to your leg. If you feed him in different positions, he will get confused.

7. Very gradually add more steps between treats, but resist the urge to go very far without reinforcement for good behavior. Remember that you are competing for your pup's attention in a very interesting environment.

8. If your dog forges ahead while you are walking, make a 180-degree turn to the right so that he doesn't get to keep pulling toward something of interest. The leash may tighten at this point, but just keep moving. Your pup will follow you. No need to say anything. When he returns to the *heel* position, immediately mark and treat.

9. Start to use your *heel* command while your pup is already walking along next to you.

Your goal is to have your dog choose to walk right next to you because it's a rewarding place to be—you shouldn't have to drag him.

Trainer Talk

Earlier we discussed the importance of controlling your pup's resources. When and where you deliver those treats is very important. For example, when you are teaching your pup to heel, you will always treat him right next to your leg in the correct *heel* position rather than reaching out to treat him when he is forging ahead. In addition, timing the delivery of the treat at the exact moment when your pup is doing what you want is an art form that you will be working on in this game and all the activities that follow.

Phase Two

When your pup is readily and consistently walking next to you with the treats luring him along, it is time to raise the bar and teach him to walk in the same place without just following the cookie. Phase One generally takes just one or two weeks to complete. It should not go on for longer than that or your pup will get dependent on just following the treats.

1. Gradually lift the treats above your pup's head by standing up a bit straighter and by bending your arm 90 degrees. With some pups you may need to work the treat up to 90 degrees in small increments, starting with it just 1 or 2 inches (2.5 or 5 cm) above the pup's nose. When you make these changes, your pup has to walk along without staring at the treat. It is your job to let him know that he will continue to be rewarded for staying in the same position.
2. Every few steps use your verbal marker and reward with a treat from your hand. Only take as many steps as your pup can handle while staying in the correct position next to your leg with your leash loose. If this is two or three, that's fine. Just mark and treat. If you take so many steps that he loses interest in you and decides to head off on his own, you will lose ground. This is a critical phase, so don't hurry.
3. Over many lessons add steps, one at a time, until you can walk a good distance before treating. I notice that many puppy raisers stop working at keeping the game fun at this point. They just assume that the pup will be good. Remember to keep your voice light and happy, smile, and reinforce the pup at intervals before he loses interest in the game. Progress very slowly as you add more steps between treats.
4. Start to use your *heel* command while you begin to move forward.

Phase Three

1. Gradually start the *heel* without a treat in your hand, although the treats should be readily accessible in your training bag. Keep your left arm bent at 90 degrees as you have been doing.
2. If your pup stays in the correct spot, use your verbal marker and deliver a treat from your bag.
3. Gradually walk a bit farther before you mark the behavior and reinforce with a cookie. If at any time your pup starts to lose interest in the game, check that you are being fun to work with. While heeling is serious business, your training session doesn't need to be serious. You may also need to mark and treat more frequently than you have been doing.

4. Now use your *heel* command before you start moving.

There is a danger at this level. The pups are generally starting to look like they understand the *heeling* game, prancing along happily next to their handlers. I notice frequently that the puppy raisers start to take the behavior for granted. Big mistake. Remember that heeling takes terrific self-control on the pup's part. You need to watch and reward consistently until your pup is at least a year old, and then on occasion after that. Any behavior that doesn't get reinforced goes away.

Heeling takes a lot of self-control on your puppy's part, so reward him consistently until he's at least a year old.

Phase Four

It's time to teach your pup to sit whenever you stop. He has likely learned that command already since pups take to it very easily. If he forgets, just show a treat a few times and raise it over his forehead until he sits. It is a good idea to use some kind of barrier at this point so that your pup sits straight, facing ahead. A wall or the back of a sofa makes a useful barrier.

Phase Five

When your pup can heel consistently at home, take your training on the road. Find a location a bit more distracting than your yard. If he is successful, gradually expand the places you work to include lots of distractions. This phase needs to progress very slowly so that your pup continues to be successful.

You can start to use your *heel* command to initiate the behavior.

Possible Challenges

For this technique to work, your dog must be food motivated—make sure that your pup works for meals.

When learning to heel, pups can either forge or lag. Forging means that the pup wants to walk in front of the handler's leg. Lagging means that the pup wants to hang back behind the handler's leg. Dogs who are allowed to forge will eventually take charge and drag you along, but you can discourage this from your first day of training.

If your pup forges, you need to react right away. If he walks any distance before you do anything, you will have a confused partner. You can do two different things.

Strategy one is to simply turn 180 degrees the minute your pup starts pulling and walk the other way. Pups pull because they want to get somewhere. Walk a distance and then try to go the original direction again. The minute the pup pulls, turn on your heel again. If you go the other way, the pup will learn that pulling doesn't work. This strategy takes terrific self-discipline since you may not make it to your destination at all for several days. If you try this approach, remember to reward your pup each time he walks nicely next to you in the correct position on a loose leash.

Strategy two is to simply back up at the first hint of a pull. The moment your pup's ear pushes ahead of your leg, quietly back up. This will turn him toward you so that he is not getting to pull you where he wants to go. Take a few steps and then just start walking forward again, which will automatically put him back at your side. Immediately reward him when he is in the correct position.

If your pup lags, he may be a bit discouraged, or he may have found something more interesting than you. Make sure that you are making your training fun and offering plenty of treats for walking next to you. Never pull on a pup who is lagging. It will always make him walk even more slowly.

Baby pups, generally between 10 and 12 weeks old, sometimes sit down when practicing the *heel*. It seems they simply get overwhelmed or confused. Don't tug or chastise the pup; just scoop him up for a bit. It might seem that this rewards him for stopping, but interestingly it never seems to keep pups from learning a fine *heel*. Once you put the pup back down, he will inevitably walk.

Exercise #15: Lie Down

Goal: Teach your dog to lie down quickly and stay down until released.
Ideal Age to Start: 11 weeks
Groundwork: Frontload the Clicker (Exercise #2) and I Can Sit (Exercise #10)
Clicker: Yes

Background

Teaching your pup to lie down is a staple of puppy training. Every pup needs to lie down when asked and stay down until released to relax or play a different game.

While learning *sit* is easy for most pups, *down* is sometimes more challenging. Lying down is a submissive posture, and some headstrong pups don't like that idea. As a result, teaching this command may require a bit more time than the things you have taught so far, and certainly more patience. Push your pup too fast and you may have a battle on your hands. Teach it in a positive way and you will have a pup who drops like a rock when you ask him to.

The clicker is particularly helpful with this command because it gives your pup

Real-Life Pups

Lauri acquired Baby Jade as a future agility prospect. In agility, trainers want the dog to lie down and spring to their feet very quickly. Dogs are taught to lie with their legs under them in a position that resembles the Sphinx. Jade was a quick learner, and in a few weeks she loved to down on just a verbal command. In fact, she would offer the behavior frequently in an effort to make Lauri give her a treat.

Teaching your pup to lie down is a staple of puppy training.

immediate feedback that you like what he has done. As usual, the precise timing of your click will help your pup understand exactly what it is that you are pleased about.

Process

Phase One

Gather up your leashed pup, your clicker, and a pocketful of good treats. Sit on the lawn or on the floor indoors. You may want to sit on your leash to keep your pup from backing up initially. Many pups think they can earn the treat by throwing it into reverse gear, and you will need both your hands for other work. In fact, three hands are useful in this game.

1. With your pup in front of you, show him a bit of food.
2. Slowly draw the food from his nose to a spot between his paws. He will try to figure out how to get it. He may sit, stand, or walk a bit. No worries. Just hold the treat on the ground. Eventually he will either play bow by dropping his front half down or he will lie all the way down. In either case, click and immediately release the treat.

    You might wonder why you click and reward the play bow. There are times it is useful to reinforce the pup when he heads in the right direction. The *down* is one of those times.
3. While your pup is lying down, offer him several treats so that he knows that position is exactly what you wanted.

4. Before he gets up on his own, gently stand him up by putting your hand under his belly. You don't want your pup to be the one to decide when the game is over. (You will learn more about releasing your pup from a command later.) Remember that you are teaching the pup to lie down right now, not to stay down.

When luring your pup with the treat, you will need to experiment with the angle of movement that works best. Some dogs will follow the treat into a *down* if the treat moves diagonally as described. Other pups do better if the treat moves from the nose straight to the ground. Still others require that you push the treat diagonally from their nose to a spot near their chest.

If you rewarded the play bow initially, you should raise the bar fairly quickly. By your second lesson with *down*, don't do anything if your pup bows. Just wait and hold your treat on the ground. He may look confused. Don't start talking. Let him think. Most pups eventually try lying down. When he does, click and treat, treat, treat. Remember to lift your pup into a standing position before he gets up on his own.

Earlier we talked about the importance of where a pup gets his cookies. This is a prime example. When you are teaching the *down*, the pup should receive all his cookies while he is in the *down* position. If you reward him after he pops up, you are teaching him that you want him to get up rather than teaching him that you love it when he lies down and relaxes. (When being rewarded for the play bow, the pup should receive his treats while bowing, not after he has stood up.)

At this level, your pup should do the *down* 30 to 50 times. Remember to talk only with the clicker and to keep your mouth very quiet.

Trainer Talk

A frequently used training term is "shaping." This is the process of breaking a complex behavior into parts and teaching each of them until the pup can do the entire behavior. When a trainer reinforces the play bow, she is shaping the *down* behavior by rewarding the first half of the motion. All teachers use the concept of shaping. All of us learned to write by learning letters, short words, and then sentences. Shaping is a powerful tool to help pups learn without excess pressure.

When luring your pup with a treat, experiment with the angle of movement that works best.

Phase Two

There are two changes at this level. First, you can start saying the *down* command. Say it *after* your pup is lying down. The pup now hears the command with no chance of getting the behavior wrong. After you say the command, click and reinforce.

It is also time for you to stand up rather than sit on the floor. Continue to lure, click, and treat as you have been doing.

Phase Three

Your pup should be comfortable with this game now. It is time to teach him to down next to you rather than in front of you since this will be his working position. You can use a barrier such a wall to help him understand that you like it when he stays at your side. Simply position the pup next to the barrier and lure him into the *down*. Find lots of different places to practice this. In this phase, start to give the command as the pup is on the way to lying down.

You can combine this game with the casual *heel* and *sit* by working along a long wall. Stop occasionally and have him either sit or down.

Phase Four

The big change now is that you are going to quit luring your pup into the *down* with food. Dogs are prone to getting particularly dependent on the lure while learning *down*.

1. Remove the treat from your hand. However, perform the exact same hand motion you have been doing to cue your pup. This is called a body cue. Having seen that motion many times, your pup will follow your hand.
2. As soon as he hits the ground, click and jackpot.

In this phase, it is a good idea to alternate between holding a lure and not holding a lure for a few sessions so that your pup doesn't think you are asking too much too fast. Then drop the lure altogether when he knows he will get his cookies when he is down.

Eventually, your pup should be able to down in increasingly distracting settings.

Phase Five

1. With your clicker and treats handy, give your *down* command along with your

body cue *before* the pup has already initiated the behavior.

2. When he plops down, click and jackpot.

Phase Six

Now it's time to wean your pup off all of your body movement.

1. Gradually shorten the distance you bend over while cueing the pup until you are not bending over at all and your hand motion is minimal.
2. Click and treat each time your pup is successful.

Your goal is to have your pup *down* on only the command word with no cueing from you. This may take up to a week of practice. If you have done each of these steps methodically, your pup will plop down. Hallelujah. Click and treat, treat, treat.

To teach your pup to stay down, feed him small bits of cookie while he is lying down.

Phase Seven

Now it is time to work on teaching your pup to stay down. As I mentioned earlier, lying down and staying down are two completely separate behaviors.

1. To teach your pup to stay down, feed him small bits of cookie while he is lying down. The pace of delivering these treats should be just fast enough to keep him in the *down* position. For twitchy pups, the delivery is rapid-fire initially. For quiet pups, there may be seconds between treats. Your goal is to deliver at a pace so that your pup continues to stay down. If he pops up, you have not made it worth his while to stay down.
2. Start to add space between treats. If you had to deliver them back to back during your first lesson, put one second between each treat. If you could wait five seconds, wait six. If your pup gets up at any time, you have asked too much too fast. I find that puppy raisers often want their pups to go from lying down for five seconds to lying down for several minutes in a heartbeat.
3. This practice will extend over several weeks and months until your pup can lie down as long as you want. At a year old, it's reasonable to expect him to lie down for up to an hour if you have taught this well.

Phase Eight

Ask your pup to down and stay down in increasingly distracting settings. Continue to click and reinforce each successful performance. When you start to work in a new setting, you may need to return to frequent cookie delivery to keep your pup in a *down*. As he becomes comfortable with performing in new places, you can wean him from the steady flow of goodies.

If your pup can't comply in a stimulating environment, back off to somewhere he can be successful. Then gradually increase the challenge.

Possible Challenges

If your pup is slow to lie down initially, try not to get frustrated. Instead, bring out your high-powered treats. Then remember to offer lots of treats once your pup decides to lie down, which he will, if you are patient. He needs to know that lying down is rewarding.

Exercise #16: Stay!

Goal: Teach your puppy to stay in one place until released while you walk away.

Ideal Age to Start: 12 weeks

Groundwork: To prepare for this game, work with your pup on the games I Can Sit (Exercise #10) and Lie Down (Exercise #15). You are ready to teach the *sit-stay* when your pup knows how to sit next to you for at least 15 seconds. You are ready to teach the *down-stay* when your pup has learned how to lie down at your side for at least 15 seconds.

Clicker: Use only for the *sit* or *down*. Just use verbal praise for the *stay*.

Background

A canine good citizen must be able to sit quietly or lie down quietly when asked to do so for a reasonable amount of time. A solid *stay* has many uses. If you begin to teach *stay* at about three months and continue to work on it slowly and sequentially until your pup is at least a year old, you will be able to have him lie down quietly while you eat dinner or sit near the door like a gentleman while guests come in.

The *stay* command is the same whether your pup is sitting or lying down. It is his job to remain in that position until you release him.

In teaching this command, you will use the verbal command earlier than in any other exercise. This is because the dog doesn't have to take action to respond to the word "stay." He just needs to stay where he is.

One last note when teaching this command: Always return to the position next to your pup before you give him a cookie. If you reward him as you walk back, there is a good chance that he will want to move toward you rather than sitting tight.

Process

Phase One

1. With your pup on leash, ask him to sit next to you. Click and reward that behavior.
2. Put the hand closest to your pup in front of his face with your fingers pointing toward the ground.
3. While you hold it there, rotate directly in front of him. Let your hand roll over.
4. Keeping your hand down, turn right back next to your pup. Make sure that you don't have any treats in your hand when you are moving out and back.
5. When you are back next to your pup, but not while you are still rotating, praise him and give him a treat from your bag while he is still seated.
6. Make sure to release him so that he knows it is okay to stand up. To do an informal release, gently place your hand under the dog's belly and tickle so that he stands up. You can also take a step forward if needed.
7. Repeat this 30 to 50 times over acouple of weeks.

Phase Two

1. Again, have your pup sit next to you. This time put your hand in front of his face just briefly rather than holding it there.
2. Then rotate right in front of him and back exactly as you did before. Make it very quick initially. This is a bit more difficult because he doesn't have that stop sign holding him in place. Remember not to give any treats when in front of your pup because this encourages him to move forward.
3. When you are back next to him, praise and give a treat.
4. If this goes well for a few tries, start to use the verbal command *stay* as you show your dog your hand. Say it firmly but remember not to sound grumpy.

    Gradually extend the time that you stand in front of your pup from a second or two to 10, 15, and then 30 seconds. Remember that you are still right in front of your pup. You can praise him while he holds the *stay* as long as this doesn't cause him to stand up.

Phase Three

1. Start the same way as in Phase Two, but now, as you step in front of your pup, move half a step back.
2. If your pup holds, make sure to praise and reinforce after you return to his side.

A well-trained dog must be able to sit quietly for a reasonable amount of time when asked to do so.

3. Over the next few weeks, gradually migrate back until you are at the end of your leash.

Each time you move farther away from your pup, shorten the time you remain there so that your pup doesn't have to work on two things at once. Always work on one variable at a time when training your dog. Once your pup is comfortable with you at a certain distance, you can extend the time you remain at that spot.

If your pup gets up when you have moved away from him, gently take him back to the location where he started the *stay* and have him sit or down on the same spot. The reason for taking the pup back to the starting place is that you don't want him to learn that it pays to wander forward. To be useful, *stay* has to mean "stay where I put you."

If your pup gets up when you have moved away from him, gently take him back to the location where he started the *stay* and have him sit or down on the same spot.

If your pup gets up consistently, he is telling you that you have moved too far away too fast. Return to a distance where he is able to be successful and then migrate away more slowly over several weeks.

Phase Four

Once your pup can hold his *stay* when seated with you at the end of his leash for at least 30 seconds, it's time to teach him to stay even if you move.
1. Start by just taking one step sideways.
2. If he stays, praise him.
3. Move a step in the other direction.
4. Return to your pup's side and reward him.

Phase Five

Start to add distractions. Ask your pup to stay in his kindergarten class when waiting for class to start. Ask your pup to stay with the kindergarten teacher standing nearby. Take him to a small shopping center or pet store and ask him to stay with strangers and carts at a safe distance. As he is successful, repeat the exercise closer to the action. Take him a variety of places to proof the *stay*.

Phase Six
Repeat these steps with your puppy in a *down*.

Phase Seven
Very gradually extend the length and the challenge of both *stays*. I knew that my young, food-crazed Sheltie Boo had this command nailed when he could hold a *stay* while I carried his dinner across the room and took my time setting it down. Take your time with training and you will have a pup with a rock-solid *stay* by at least a year old.

Trainer Talk
As you train your pup, you will very gradually add distractions so that he can successfully perform each command even when there are lots of things going on around him. This process is known in training lingo as "proofing." I think of it as having the pup *prove* he knows his job. I know that I have proofed a puppy's stay when he can stay put even when there are other puppies or dogs running nearby. This takes lots of practice.

Possible Challenges
The biggest challenge with teaching *stay* is generally the human side of the equation. Here is what commonly happens: The handler asks the dog to sit or down and then stay. When she moves away, the pup gets up. The handler returns, asks the dog to sit or down, and gives him a treat when he complies. This teaches the pup that breaking the *stay* is a good deal. To avoid this message, don't treat your pup if you need to put him back in the correct position. Just give the command neutrally, repeat the *stay*, and move away to a spot your pup can handle. I know. I know. Generally I say not to repeat commands, but in this case you need to remind the pup what you were working on because several seconds have passed while you put him back in position.

Exercise #17: Life on the Long Line
Goal: Your dog comes consistently when called in the house or yard.
Ideal Age to Start: 12 weeks (or earlier if your pup shows a propensity for ignoring you)
Groundwork: Back-and-Forth *Recall* (Exercise #5) and informal *recall* games around the house
Clicker: Yes

Background
Many pups are good about coming when the game is carefully structured (like the *recall* game you have already played). But often when the pup thinks he is free, he will suddenly develop a mind of his own and choose to run the other way when called. This can happen when the pup feels the first surge of teenage hormones, or earlier with independent-minded pups.

This game is designed to teach your pup that it is always a better decision to come right to you than to do something else. It eliminates any sense of choice that a pup might have about ignoring you. Obviously, it must be used over several months to make sure that the lesson is completely internalized by the pup.

For this game bring your long line, a piece of equipment we discussed in the equipment chapter but have not yet used. The long line is a light piece of material (commonly cotton, twine, nylon, or cord) between 20 and 30 feet (6 and 9 m) in length. Choose the lightest-weight long line possible to hold your youngster. This is because you want your dog to be as unaware of the line as possible. It is helpful to put knots in the line at intervals so that it doesn't just slide under your foot when you step on it.

The long line is one of your most powerful training tools and seriously underused by most puppy raisers. It allows you to influence your pup from a distance, which is essential when he goes through the inevitable free-spirited phases. Remember that once a pup learns to ignore you, retraining is an uphill battle.

Many trainers put on a long line the day they bring home a new pup and don't take it off when they are outside until they know with 100 percent certainty that their pup will come when called. There is nothing wrong with this approach. Since you have been so busy with other things, I have deferred this process for a few weeks. Generally this is fine because there is a honeymoon period during which our pups adore us and adolescence has not clicked in. However, the first time your pup shows any inclination to choose another activity over coming to you, bring out the long line. I try not to shriek during puppy classes when puppy raisers confess that their pup has been refusing to come for weeks and they have done nothing.

Process

Phase One

Take your pup, with both leash and long line attached to his buckle collar, into a fenced area that he is likely to enjoy exploring. Make sure that your pockets are filled with good treats.

1. Make a show of taking off the leash so that the pup thinks he is free, but put your foot on the end of the long line.
2. Let your pup drift away. When he hits the end of the line, he will stop in surprise. Keep your foot on the line and call him. You can have food in your hand at this point.

Teach your dog to consistently come to you whether he's in the house or the yard.

3. When he gets to you, click or use your marker word and offer a series of small treats.
4. Repeat this game in a variety of locations.

Phase Two

1. Play the game the same way, but now call your pup without food in your hands. This is important because some pups learn to come only if they see the reward. You want your pup to come whether he sees the reward or not.
2. When your pup comes directly to you even though the cookie is not visible, throw a party.

Trainer Talk

Handlers cause some *recall* problems by inadvertently doing one of the three *nevers*. Never #1: Don't call your pup for anything that he thinks is unpleasant. Never #2: Don't call your pup to punish him for something. Never #3: Resist calling him if there is any chance he won't come. Do any of these even once, and your pup will be anxious when you call. You can significantly set back your progress if you let your pup think that coming to you is anything but joyous.

Phase Three

Gradually expand the locations where you play the game. Include anywhere that you might need to call your pup. For example, I play this game with my pups out in the front yard. Although they are never purposefully loose in this unfenced area, what if one slipped out when a guest arrived? Obviously, you must be careful that the long line stays firmly under your foot if you are in a high-risk location.

When you decide to remove the long line based on your pup's reliability when coming, do it gradually so that he is never sure whether it is on or off. If he backslides even once by deciding not to come, put it back on and use it for several weeks so that he that he doesn't have an option to take off. Remember to reward generously when he chooses you.

Real-Life Pups

It is especially important for future assistance dogs to come when called because their future owners depend on them to perform important tasks such as picking up dropped keys or turning a light switch off. When the puppy raiser for a little guy named Powell told me that her pup was already showing an independent streak at ten weeks, we brought out the long line. For the next two weeks Powell was never loose in the yard without the long line. The handler played the game described here with him. In addition, any time she wanted the pup, she went and stood on the end of the line before she called. After this practice, the handler reported that the pup was very responsive about coming when called. She is keeping the long line handy because she knows she may need it again as he becomes an adolescent.

Possible Challenges

When you are playing the long line game, you may encounter one problem. Some pups will arrive at the end of the leash either at a stroll or a run and then just contently sniff in a circle around you, rather than coming back when you call. To deal with this, I have recently adapted an interesting strategy described by trainer Dale Stavroff in his book *Let the Dog Decide.*

If your pup does not return to you, drop a big piece of food near your feet. If your pup approaches and eats it, click and drop another piece. Don't reach out to grab or pet the pup. If he starts to walk off, drop another piece. When he returns to get that, click and drop another. Every time the pup starts to wander away, drop a cookie. Each time he comes back to you to eat it, click and reinforce again. He is learning that staying close to you is much better than exploring alone. Once he is comfortable with hanging out near you, start backing away one step at a time. Every time he chooses to follow you, drop another cookie, click, and reward. Just stay quiet during this game and let the pup decide to follow you. Once he is responding quickly to this strategy, return to the original game.

Exercise #18: Release

Goal: Teach your pup to recognize when he is "off duty."
Ideal Age to Start: 5 months
Groundwork: Your pup will be working on all of the commands you have taught thus far. You will use this new command to tell your pup when he is done with an exercise and that he can relax for a moment.
Clicker: Yes

Background

It is very important while you are working with your pup that you communicate clearly to him when he is working and when he is just relaxing with you. The most common mistake I see puppy raisers make is this: They ask their pup to do something such as sit. They tell the pup he is good and give a treat. The puppy raiser then turns her attention elsewhere. The pup, left to his own devices, either flops to the ground or gets up on his

The *release* command teaches a dog that he is done with an exercise and can relax.

Trainer Talk

When you are in a puppy training class, the etiquette is different from everyday life. Normally we are taught to watch the teacher. That is true if your puppy class teacher is demonstrating something, of course, but during most of the class your attention should be on your puppy. I often see handlers come into class with their pups well under control. After they ask their pups to lie down, they start chatting. Their pups comply, grow bored, get up, and wander away. The pups have learned that they are calling the shots regarding when the game ends. If you can't watch your pup, release him and let him relax quietly near you.

own. The result is that the pup learns that he, not his handler, decides when he is done working, which is not what you want.

As a good teacher for your pup, you must remember that you are in charge of what he does, how long he does it, and when he is free not to do it anymore. This takes a lot of concentration. We often say that training sessions for pups should be short because they have a limited attention span. We might add that lessons for pups should be short because people have a short attention span.

Up to this point, I have been having you release your pup informally after each command. I did this by asking you to stand your pup up after he did an exercise such as *sit* or *down.* Now you will start teaching the pup a new command so that he knows he is on a coffee break. I saved this command until now because you had so many other things to teach.

After your pup learns the *release* command, one of two things will always happen during training. Either you will follow a command with another command, or you will release your pup. For example, you might ask your dog to heel and then follow this with an instruction to wait at a curb. Or you might give a command such as *stay.* After you reward your pup, you would release him before asking him to stay a second time. When you use the *release* command during a training session, the pup's break may only be a few seconds long. When you use the *release* at the end of a training session, it may mean that your pup is off for hours.

When you release your pup, have him stand up. Puppy raisers often ask me why they need to have the pup stand up if he is already comfortable lying down. The answer is that you need to make it clear to the pup that he is off duty. If you simply let him lie down once you have given this command, you have no way of knowing if he knows that he is on a break. If he chooses to lie down after completing the *release*, that is certainly fine.

On a final note, there is debate about what word to use for this command. Most folks use the word "okay." The problem is that "okay" is such a common word that dogs hear it all the time and may not always understand what you have in mind. Just to play it safe, I encourage the use of another word, such as "release."

Process

Phase One
1. With your puppy on leash, have him sit or down. Click and treat that behavior.
2. Gently grasp his collar with the hand closest to him.
3. Step forward with your foot farthest away from the pup and lure until he stands up.
4. Mark with your clicker and reward him.
5. Repeat 30 to 50 times over a number of sessions.

   Once your pup is standing, he is free to walk near you without pulling on the leash. He may sit or lie down on his own. Although he is off duty, he doesn't get to go wild and run around you because he is still on leash.

Phase Two
Repeat the exercise and add your verbal command after he has stood up.

Phase Three
Play the game again and use your command as he is standing.

Phase Four
Give your command while he is seated or down. If he responds by standing, click and throw a small party.

Possible Challenges
As you already gathered, the biggest challenge with this command is simply remembering to do it. Remember that whenever you are working with your pup, you are responsible for giving the commands, and you are also responsible for communicating when the activity is over. Imagine what would happen if you went to work and no one ever said when it was over. You would just wander off whenever you felt like it. Pretty soon work wouldn't seem very important. This is exactly the same for your pup.

Real-Life Pups
I had a student in an agility class with a talented young Labrador. The only problem was that the dog wouldn't stay on the start line, which is essential to doing well in agility. Finally, I noticed that when the handler left his dog in a pen between runs, he always told the dog to lie down. As he walked away, the dog always got up on his own. This was a classic case of a dog who did not know when he was on or off duty. Our fix began when the handler stopped giving commands he was not going to reinforce. Then we taught the dog when he was on duty by reviewing the *stay* command and when he was off duty by teaching him the *release* command. Soon we had a dog who knew his job at the beginning of an agility run.

Exercise #19: Give Me That

Goal: Teach your pup to give you items that he has picked up.
Ideal Age to Start: 5 months (although you can start earlier if your pup is a sneak thief)
Groundwork: It is ideal if you have played Life on the Long Line (Exercise #17), but that is not essential to teach this command.
Clicker: No

Background

Puppies naturally want to pick up objects, carry them around, and eventually settle down for a good chew. This tendency doubles for retrieving breeds, whose genes tell them to pick up anything that isn't bolted down. Your pup has no idea about the difference between a stuffed toy that you bought for him and that pair of sheepskin slippers you just purchased.

When raising a pup, it is a good idea, of course, to store items you want to protect out of his reach. However, he will inevitably pick up the television remote or your favorite socks one day. You have two choices at this moment. The natural, but incorrect, reaction is to shriek and then either call the puppy or chase him. A pup whose *recall* is not totally reliable will likely choose not to come because you have just startled him by raising your voice: *No way am I coming to you. You sound crazy.* If you take the alternate route and chase the pup, you have just initiated every puppy's favorite game—keep-away! You are actively teaching him to run away from you when he has a prize.

The best solution is to teach your pup that you will "buy" anything that he picks up. If he either hands you the object or drops it on the floor, he will earn a treat.

In classes, puppy raisers are sometimes resistant to this idea. They worry that they are rewarding their pup for picking up things he shouldn't. I have bad news. Pups will pick up things they shouldn't. You can either get a stolen item back in a positive way or create a little monster who grabs things and runs or chews them behind the sofa. It's much better to teach your pup to trust you so that you can see when something has gone awry.

There is no clicker in this game because you will actually be trading the object the pup has picked up for a cookie. In addition, there is a good chance your pup will decide to grab a household item at a moment when you don't have a clicker in hand.

Process

Phase One

In the beginning, you'll control the situation by keeping your pup on leash and selecting the objects you will let him pick up. Make sure that your pockets are filled with high-powered treats.

1. Sit on the couch or on the floor with your pup. Sit or stand on the leash to free up both your hands.
2. Offer your pup an object you know he will like. If he has beloved toys, this is a great place to start. If not, use any object he will take in his mouth.
3. Hand him the toy and let him hold it for a few seconds. Then gently reach out and grasp the toy at the same time you offer a treat.
4. As soon as he releases the toy, mark the release with "yes!" and hand him the treat. After he

eats, give him the toy back and repeat the game. If he loses interest in the toy, play with him between repetitions. Bounce the toy around on the floor until he takes it in his mouth. Then let him hold it for a few seconds before you trade it for a treat.

5. Over several sessions repeat the game 30 to 50 times. It is fine to switch objects each session as long as your pup is interested in holding each item in his mouth.

If you are using your pup's toy, give him the toy to keep at the end of your training. If you are using a different object, leave him with one of his toys.

Phase Two

Play the same game but change locations. Keep your pup on leash. You may start using your *give* command just after your pup releases the object.

Phase Three

There are two changes now. First, start using your command as your pup is opening his mouth to release the object. Second, put your pup's long line on and sit or stand on it so that you don't have to use your hands. This starts to simulate a situation in which the pup could dart away with a prize.

1. If your pup decides to run off with the toy, let him hit the end of the line; this teaches him that he can't get very far if he runs.
2. When he glances at you, drop a chunk of food by your foot as you did with the long line game in Life on the Long Line (Exercise #17).
3. When he returns, let him eat it while you pick up the toy.
4. Then immediately restart the Give Me That game as you have been playing it. Make it lots of fun, with plenty of cookies for giving the toy to you.

Phase Four

1. Play the same game, but start using the *give* command before your pup starts to let go.
2. When he gives you the object, celebrate and reward generously.

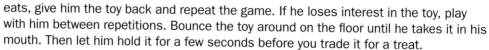

Real-Life Pups

My young Labrador had a sock obsession. While I was putting one on or if one fell from the dryer, she would grab it and run. While not surprising for a dog bred to pick things up, the cute factor wore off fairly quickly since the sock often ended up in the yard or went missing altogether. When she didn't outgrow the behavior, I began the Give Me That process. I filled my pockets with high-value cookies and then attached a long line. Next, I tossed a sock and followed the process. In a few days, she saw socks less as a prize and more as a means to earn a treat. Once socks were no longer on her grab-and-run list, she did start stealing leather slippers, but I am sure you can figure out what training came next.

Phase Five

Now we are going to set the pup up in a more realistic situation. Make sure that you have your best treats handy in your pocket.

1. Attach your pup to his long line and let him drag it. This is a safeguard in case he decides to take off. Go about your business for a few minutes with your pup nearby.
2. Then "accidentally" drop something that you know your pup will want. In our house, socks, underwear, and well-seasoned slippers are the hot puppy items.
3. Walk a short distance away and try not to stare at the pup.
4. If he picks up the object, crouch down immediately. If the pup comes to you, praise him. Use his *give* command.
5. Mark and reward, reward, reward if he complies.

Dogs, particularly retrieving breeds, naturally want to pick up objects and use them as chew toys.

Possible Challenges

Sometimes at this last phase, a pup will think that he is free and make a dash for freedom with a prize. It is your job to teach him that it simply never works to try to get away and that there are cookies close to you. Here is a plan, adapted from trainer Dale Stavroff's book *Let the Dog Decide*, if your pup decides to go on a tear with something he shouldn't have:

1. Walk to the end of the long line and stand on it. Resist the urge to say anything.
2. Pretend that you have no interest in the pup in the hope that he will take off again. If he does, the long line will stop him.
3. When he looks at you, look away again. This gives him a chance to run again, which is a good thing in this controlled situation. If he bolts, just stand quietly on the long line.

Trainer Talk

Trainers often talk of "setting up" a pup. This refers to creating an artificial situation that gives you a chance to teach your pup a correct behavior. In this game, we set up a situation in which we hope the pup will pick up something inappropriate while we are watching so that we can make sure to react in a way that teaches rather than frightens the pup. There are many opportunities in training for setups. For example, teaching your dog to sit nicely when a guest comes in your house works much better if the guest is not a surprise.

4. If he doesn't run or quits trying to run, use your marker word "yes!" and drop a piece of food by your foot as you did during your long line work earlier. When he approaches and eats, pick up the desired object. Start to play the game again with plenty of cookies for letting go of the "toy."

5. When you end the game, always leave the pup with something appropriate that he values.

Reward your dog profusely when he relinquishes an item to you upon request.

Occasionally, pups may be overly possessive of toys or objects they find. This can become a serious problem and must be dealt with directly. If your pup refuses to give up a toy (or a food bowl), growls, or bites, even you if are offering a treat, this should raise a red flag. Most dogs can learn to get over this in time, but it is best to seek help from a professional trainer if you are confronted with behavior that makes you feel threatened.

Exercise #20: You Called?

Goal: Your dog comes consistently when called in the house or yard.
Ideal Age to Start: 6 months (or earlier if your pup is ignoring you)
Groundwork: Back-and-Forth *Recall* (Exercise #5) and Life on the Long Line (Exercise #17)
Clicker: Yes

Background

In this chapter, you played two formal *recall* games. You have also been working on teaching your pup to love coming to you with dozens of informal *recalls* each day. As you remember, you should be calling him when you know he will come and treating him lavishly from the bowls of goodies you have placed everywhere for that purpose.

As your pup matures, he will naturally test limits. Think teenager. This makes it especially important that you continue to work consciously on your *recall*.

This game starts in the house with your pup loose and then moves outdoors with him on the leash and long line.

Process

Phase One

1. Fill your pocket with high-value treats and have your clicker ready.
2. Wait until your pup is relaxing a few feet (m) away from you but not paying attention to you.
3. Say his name quietly and add "come." He has learned this command in the other games. He will get up and come to you, expecting a reward.
4. When he gets to you (close enough to grasp his collar if you wanted), click and treat, treat, treat. It may take him a few repetitions to figure out the game. Be patient and don't start talking. If you have laid a good foundation, he will respond.
5. Play this game several times over several days.
   During this phase, don't repeat his name or the command. Speak quietly but cheerfully. It is your pup's job to listen to you, not yours to try to get his attention.
   When he is coming to you happily and consistently, move on to the next stage.

Phase Two

1. When your pup is out of sight in the house, say his name and the word "come."
2. When he comes to you, click and throw a party with treats. Remember, this is just a game. Keep it light and fun. Soon he'll come running every time he hears his name and the command.
3. Play this hundreds of times during your pup's first year, and change your location frequently. Set a goal for the number of *recalls* each day so that your work on this doesn't fade. Twenty or more times a day is very reasonable.

Phase Three

When your pup is reliable about coming in the house, it's time to add mild distractions.

1. Keep your pup under control so that he can't make a mistake. Take him for a walk on his regular leash in a quiet place.
2. Before he gets too distracted, use his name and your *come* command.
3. When he comes, click and treat. If by chance he doesn't come, reel him in gently and give him lots of treats. If he doesn't come the second time you call, find a place with fewer things of interest and increase the value of the treats.

Phase Four

When your pup comes consistently with mild distractions, up the ante by letting him get seriously distracted.

1. Allow him to start sniffing. Then call him using his name and your *come* command.
2. When he comes to you, click and give him several treats. If he doesn't come, reduce the level of distractions.

3. Continue to take him different places with more distractions. Don't start repeating his name or the command. If he doesn't respond immediately, reel him in and treat him. Never chastise him. Just let him see that you have stuff that is too wonderful to ignore. Soon you'll have a dog running back to you on his name no matter what is going on around him.
4. Work with your pup until you can call him even with other dogs running nearby.

Phase Five
Now play the game on a long line.
1. Start with letting him get approximately 15 feet (4.6 m) from you; then call him.
2. If that goes well several times, gradually lengthen the amount of line you give him. For pups who struggle with the *recall*, I use a line of up to 50 feet (15 m) in the final stages.
3. Click each time your pup returns and reward generously.

Phase Six
Play the game with your pup loose in a fenced area. If he doesn't respond even a single time, put the long line back on. When he does respond and race back to you, tell him that he is best pup ever.

Real-Life Pups
A young couple brought a year-old rescued Papillon to my class. He was an exuberant, bright young pup. According to his owners, he was a delight in every way except he often refused to come at home. I quickly saw this behavior in class when the couple tried to attach his leash and he started dancing just out of reach. When a hand was extended, he would jump back and grin. His new owners wanted to launch on a *recall* program, but first they had to find a way to get him on leash to even start training. They found that they could get him into a small exercise pen with a small meal. Once enclosed, they could snap on his leash without calling him.

Once he was leashed, they started playing the exercise in which they grasped his collar, clicked, and treated. They played this multiple times a day for two weeks. In addition, they resisted the urge to ever call him around the house and give him an opportunity to refuse. After the collar game, they began playing all the *recall* games, starting with calling him back and forth in the hallway (Back-and-Forth Recall, Exercise #5). He has made great strides and comes reliably in the house now. He is intermittently rewarded with high-value treats when he comes up and allows his owner to grasp his collar. He is still wearing the long line when he goes into the yard, to ensure that he doesn't regress.

Trainer Talk

Many folks choose to rescue an older pup or dog rather than starting with a young pup. This is a good trend because many dogs are relinquished to shelters or rescue groups. If you rescue a dog, he may arrive with well-established habits. Once he has a few days to settle in, start to work with him on the exercises in this book. Even if he has some baggage, he is capable of learning. Start at the beginning and progress as you would with a pup, although you may need to adjust the pacing. Resist the urge to spoil him or fail to teach him because he had a challenging start. I have watched many rescue dogs arrive in obedience and agility classes looking apprehensive. A few months later, they are unrecognizable as they work joyfully with their handlers.

Possible Challenges

There are two common challenges with the *recall*. The first is the pup who simply ignores his handler. If this is your pup, return to Life on the Long Line (Exercise #17). Make sure to play the game included under Possible Challenges until your pup responds consistently. Then progress to this exercise.

A second challenge is the pup who learns to play keep-away. This happens because the handler grabs the pup when he comes and then does something to the pup that he dislikes. This may be as simple as snapping on the leash, which the pup perceives as ending his freedom. You can avoid teaching him to play keep-away by training this exercise and by following two other guidelines.

1. If you need to do something that is awful in the pup's mind, such as trimming his nails, gently go and get him. Do not call him.
2. Add one step to this game the first time your pup shows any hint of playing keep-away. Before you work on calling him, teach him that having you hold his collar is good. Do this by gently grasping his collar, clicking, and delivering a treat. Then release him. This teaches him that letting you "catch" him results in a good thing and he will get to go free afterward. Repeat this for several days. When you transition to calling him as described, grasp his collar before you click each time he comes. Then reinforce and let him go.

Chapter 9
Socialization and Confidence Building

Exercise #21: Meet the Goblins (Physical Objects)

Goal: Teach your pup that the world is a safe place.
Ideal Age to Start: 8 weeks
Groundwork: Introduction to walking on the leash and wearing a collar
Clicker: Yes, at Phase Two

Background

The world can be a scary place for a dog. Their canine brain does not come wired to deal with a world filled with vacuums, trash cans, big trucks, big hats, things that flap, hairdryers, and hundreds of other potentially frightening objects.

Socialization starts when a pup is still with his mom. If you are selecting a pup from a breeder, make sure to ask about the experiences the pups have had. Starting at about three weeks, pups should be exposed to lots of friendly people, be given chances to romp in the yard, and experience different sounds.

As soon as you bring your pup home, it becomes your job to actively introduce him to things he is likely to encounter in the world. It is essential that you introduce him in a positive way that helps him think, "Hey, I can handle that." The dog training term for systematically encouraging a pup to interact with his world is called "socialization." Some writers use the term "socialization" to refer only to dog-to-dog interactions. My use of the term includes other dogs, people, and objects.

Dogs who are not adequately socialized are likely to grow up with fear issues. They might panic at a rolling trash can, dread trips in the car, or react fearfully in the presence of a new person. If there is only one activity that you do with your dog from this book, Meet the Goblins is the most important because it will allow your dog to move easily and happily in the world.

The process of socialization has changed drastically in recent years. Not too long ago pups were kept at home for many months, until they had their final shots. But scientists and trainers have come to believe that socialization has the most

Systematically training your dog to interact with his world is called socialization.

Make sure to get your pup out and about during his first months at home.

impact on a dog's confidence before he is 16 weeks old. Some animal behaviorists think that this critical period ends even earlier, at about 12 weeks. Whatever the exact date, the pressure is on to get your pup out and about during those first months at home. The challenge is that you must balance important socialization opportunities with potential health concerns. Pups are not fully protected from their vaccines until their final puppy shots at about four months. This is a good conversation for you and your vet. Most professional trainers and folks who participate in organized dog sports are opting for extensive socialization with young pups, although until the pup has had his final shots they avoid places where they might encounter unknown dogs.

This is not to say that socialization should end after the pup is older than 16 weeks. Pups, like children, should interact with a world that gradually expands as they mature.

There is one other important note: Socialization opportunities must provide the appropriate level of stimulation for pups. For example, a walk in a quiet strip mall would be perfect for most ten-week-old pups, but a walk on a noisy city street would be over the top and would scare rather than help the pup. In Appendix I, I've included a table of the types of socialization opportunities that are at the correct level for most pups of varying ages. It is based on what we do with assistance dog pups to get them prepared for a work life that may include any environment. If you follow this plan, you will prepare your pup for anything an active life might present.

Real-Life Pups

Week 1

The first morning Jade woke up at Lauri and Richard's home, the process of socializing began. It started with a steady stream of friends who came over to meet the pup. Each visitor sat on the floor while petting and playing with her. Lauri's goal was to teach from day one that other people are her friends.

Within a day, Lauri snapped Jade's leash on and they launched their first adventure outside the house. Lauri had pockets filled with Jade's dry breakfast food. Since Lauri is an agility teacher, the agility field was a natural destination. Jade met her first goblin quickly. It was an orange plastic cone that Lauri uses to number the agility equipment. Jade eyed it cautiously. Lauri leaned down and put a small pile of food near the base and let Jade choose to approach. Because she had not had another meal, hunger won out and she walked over to snack. Next she noticed a wing on a jump. Lauri placed a few treats next to it. Jade ran up to eat them. The game went on. When she looked at anything, whether it concerned her or just interested her, Lauri reached in and put a pile of treats at the base of the object. Jade thought it was a fine game. Over the course of this first week, owner and pup took similar trips to the garage, the shed, and the barn. It was all about discovery.

Week 2

During Jade's second week at home, Lauri and Jade continued their walks, gradually expanding their range around the property and exposing Jade to new objects such as the wheelbarrow and a small wooden bridge. They also walked on a quiet lane next to the property.

At separate sessions, Lauri introduced the clicker. Jade now knew that the sound of the clicker meant that Lauri liked what she was doing. By the end of this week, Lauri could use it to communicate with her about anything.

Week 3

During week three, when Jade was 11 weeks old, Lauri began to use the clicker on socialization outings. During this week, the game changed from Meet the Goblins to Touch the Goblins. When approaching objects that Jade was already familiar with, Lauri watched to see if she would touch them with her nose or paw. If she did, Lauri would click the touch and put her treats at the base of the object. The clicker told her clearly that her handler liked what she was doing. For new objects that she encountered, Lauri continued to just place her treats at the base of the object until Jade was clearly relaxed.

Week 11

During week 11, Lauri and Jade also began taking more trips in the car. Without such a large property, Lauri would have started this a week earlier, but her property presented so much to do that she didn't find it necessary. They went to the bank and walked up to the ATM. Lauri stood outside small stores with Jade on the ground. Although she was not crazy about the car, Jade seemed to enjoy the outings. Of course, there were special treats on each field trip.

Week 12

During week 12, the focus of the game changed to Interacting with the Goblins. Lauri looked for opportunities for Jade to touch, climb on, or make noise with different objects. In most cases, Lauri lured her onto different objects like a balance disc, trash can lid, and low teeter-totter with a treat. Once she was on or in the object, Lauri clicked and treated there.

Weeks 13 to 16

Weeks 13 through 16, Lauri and Jade began to travel more extensively. Richard joined them for family weekend outings. They visited friends at their homes and strolled in a small shopping center. The feed store became a favorite destination. At each location, Lauri hung out until Jade saw people in hats, with beards, and pushing noisy carts. When they met friendly folks, Lauri allowed Jade to meet and greet. Lauri continued to click and reinforce her for interacting with objects such as the feed store scale.

By 16 weeks, Jade was a puppy of the world. Lauri has, of course, continued to add new places and more stimulating environments as she matured. But I feel confident that Jade will be able to take any goblins she might encounter in stride.

Pups should interact with a world that gradually expands as they mature.

Process

Phase One

1. Put your pup on leash with a flat collar. Fill your pocket with treats. These can be part of his regular food if he eats it happily.
2. Take a walk around your yard. The walk is all about discovery. Let your pup just wander and look at things. When he looks at something with interest, put a few pieces of food at the base of the object. Let your pup enjoy the snack.
3. Continue your walk. If your pup reacts with concern to something he sees, put your treats down nearby and let him eat there. If he just notices something, do exactly the same. If your pup doesn't look at an object, just pass it by. Do not force him to do anything that makes him uncomfortable. This is very important. You will hurt your relationship with him if you try to force the issue. Let him choose to go close to earn the food.
4. The next day take a walk in a different part of the yard. Put treats on the ground near any object your dog notices, whether his interest is neutral or anxious.

Trainer Talk

Many pups experience two fear periods even if they have been well socialized. The first commonly occurs at around eight weeks. During this period, things that the pup has taken in stride may become goblins. A new person, a loud noise, or anything unexpected evokes a reaction from hesitancy to overt fear. Fearfulness or avoidance of new things sometimes rears its head again at around 16 weeks. Occasionally pups show a bit of fear again at about a year.

If your pup experiences these fear periods, isolation is not the answer. Continue to take him out and about to places that are familiar, but don't push new places until the period passes. Also, remember not to coddle your pup when he reacts fearfully, as this will reinforce the behavior. The good news is that the fear periods are usually short. Pups generally return to their joyful behavior within a week.

5. Gradually expand your walks each day to new places in your neighborhood. Add trips to safe places. I find small strip malls that are not too busy perfect for a short walk, and pet-friendly stores are perfect for an outing. Remember to keep your pockets full of treats so that when your pup sees new objects there will be a reward for approaching them.

While your pup is in this discovery phase, make sure that you are also frontloading the clicker as described in Frontload the Clicker (Exercise #2). You will want to use it in the next phase of Meet the Goblins.

Phase One should take about two weeks.

Phase Two

When your pup clearly recognizes that going up to a new object will pay off, it is time to up the ante. Your goal now is to reward him for actually touching objects.

1. Carry your clicker and your treats. Remember to keep your treats in a bag or a readily available pocket. Don't carry the treats in your hand because pups get dependent on this and may refuse to work later unless they see the bribe.
2. Take off on a walk as you have been doing daily. When your pup notices an object,

When introducing your dog to physical objects, your goal is to reward him for touching the item in a variety of locations.

don't do anything. Just remain quiet. However, the minute he touches something, click and put a small pile of treats on the ground near the object. Remember that the timing on your click is very important. The click needs to occur simultaneously with the pup touching the object.

3. Continue your walk and repeat the same sequence. Wait for your pup to touch an object, click exactly when the touch occurs, and deliver your treats on the ground.
4. Again, repeat this game in a variety of locations that are very gradually more stimulating.

Phase Three

Keep adding field trips for your pup. Try not to let a day pass without getting him out and about for even a few minutes. Gradually expand his experiences to include everything he will encounter in his life, from gas stations to watching people swimming to meeting people in flapping coats and carrying umbrellas. Each good field trip can provide your pup with a variety of experiences. Remember that places your pup might encounter unknown dogs would be inappropriate before he has had his final puppy shots.

I hope I have made the point that every dog needs socialization to grow up healthy. One additional note: This is even more important for breeds originally developed to guard people, livestock, or property. These breeds may be naturally suspicious of strangers and act aloof. The more time you invest in socializing such dogs, the bigger the payoff.

Possible Challenges

The biggest challenge of this game is simply finding the time to play it daily. Remember that if you have to make a choice, socialization trumps training. A pup who is relaxed in the world can always learn. A pup who is fearful because he didn't have adequate experience in the world is an unhappy and sometimes dangerous animal.

Exercise #22: Off to Kindergarten

Goal: Socialize your pup with other pups and people.

Ideal Age to Start: 9 weeks or the age your local puppy kindergarten establishes

Groundwork: Your pup has been introduced to the collar and leash and you have found a well-run kindergarten puppy class.

Clicker: Use for practice in class with basic commands.

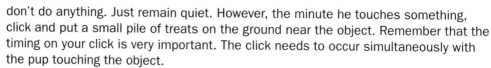

Real-Life Pups

Occasionally pups are a bit shy in a kindergarten class. They may have missed some early socialization, or maybe they just have a shy personality. If your pup is anxious or hangs back, never force interactions. Let him watch the games until he relaxes. When he is ready, start to work with him and let him interact with another quiet pup that the teacher selects.

Puppy kindergarten helps dogs work on basic manners, play games, and learn basic commands.

Background

In the past ten years, puppy kindergarten has become an institution in the dog training world. It is likely you have at least one option for taking your pup to school and possibly several choices in your neighborhood. If you can, visit more than one of the classes before you bring your pup home. Some kindergarten programs are nothing more than puppy playtime. Others do a better job of combining play periods with important puppy lessons. Here are things to watch for in a class:

- The teacher's training style should be positive, as I've described in this book. If the teacher incorporates the use of the clicker, that's even better.
- The teacher should show comfort in dealing with different breeds and types of pups.
- The class should offer opportunities to work on basic manners, games, and beginning commands. For example, learning not to pull on the leash or jump on people is perfect.
- All the pups should have time off leash to socialize with other pups of similar size and temperament. Pups must never be allowed to intimidate or boss each other.
- The teacher should intervene if a pup acts inappropriately.

Process

Simply attend your class regularly and follow the teacher's direction. If at any time you feel uncomfortable with an activity, just ask to sit it out.

Trainer Talk

An important part of early socialization is teaching your pup to interact appropriately with other pups and dogs. However, I do not recommend dog parks because you cannot predict the behavior of other dogs. One bad scare from another dog can stay with your pup his entire life.

The best play partners are similar-sized pups. If you have friends with pups, make puppy play dates. During their games pups should always be supervised so that one pup doesn't dominate the other. No pup should be held down on his back for more than a few seconds. If that happens, just gently pull the top dog off. If the top pup is yours, remove him from the game regularly by picking up his leash (which you have kept attached) and allowing him to cool his jets before going back to play.

While playing is essential for a pup to learn appropriate interactions with other canines, it is possible for pups to become excessively focused on other dogs. This is known as "dog distracted." To prevent this, let your pup play with his leash on his flat collar. Encourage him to stop playing and come to you at regular intervals during the game. The leash will help catch him if necessary. Treat, treat, treat when he comes to you and then release him to play again.

Possible Challenges

If you live outside of town, you may need to travel. This is a worthwhile activity unless you have friends with young dogs and can create your own kindergarten.

Exercise #23: Meet the Noise Goblins

Goal: Teach your pup to stay calm in a noisy environment so that he can continue to pay attention to you.

Ideal Age to Start: 9 weeks

Groundwork: Start with introducing your pup to physical objects in Meet the Goblins (Exercise #21).

Clicker: No

Background

Our modern world produces some noises that can worry a pup. In Exercise #21: Meet the Goblins, we discussed how pups don't automatically understand the howl of the hairdryer, the backfire of a truck, or hundreds of other loud sounds. Pups who don't learn to accept a wide range of noises can live anxious lives and possibly put themselves in danger if they bolt away from home when they are startled.

Interestingly, certain types of dogs are more concerned about sounds than others. They are said to be "sound sensitive." Herding breeds, such as Border Collies and Shelties, are particularly prone to fear of certain noises. However, virtually any breed can have individuals who dive under the bed when the food processor whines or a car backfires.

Sound sensitivity can rear its head during the classic eight-week and four-month fear periods, but it can pop up later too. I have seen some dogs react fearfully to noises for the first time between nine months and a year old.

As with our previous Meet the Goblins game, during which we introduced pups to a wide variety of physical objects, it is possible to introduce dogs to sounds in a positive way that helps them to take unexpected noises in stride. Clearly there is no way to present every sound a dog might encounter, but you can introduce dozens in your home and neighborhood.

It is important to understand that fear of noises is directly related to distance from the offending sound. For example, a pup may be fine with the vacuum if it is in another room but be very anxious if he is in the same room. This concept will guide your approach to this game.

Some dogs are more sensitive to sounds than others, like herding breeds.

Real-Life Pups

Right off the bat, Lauri encountered an interesting challenge with her baby Border Collie Jade. When Lauri started to introduce her to the clicker during her first week in the house, Jade showed that she was uncomfortable with even that tiny sound. When Lauri clicked, she crouched down anxiously. This was a clear message that she was sound sensitive. As an experienced trainer, Lauri knew she would have to do extensive work with sounds to make Jade comfortable in the world.

Exploring the world of sounds became part of their daily routine. As you read in Chapter 7, Lauri solved the issue with the clicker by muffling the sound in her pocket until Jade got used to it. Next she introduced the hairdryer. Lauri left Jade loose so that the pup could pick a distance that was comfortable rather than feeling trapped. Lauri loaded her pockets with food. When she turned on the hairdryer, Jade approached Lauri and the hairdryer tentatively. Lauri immediately gave her treats from her hand. She repeated this game over the course of several days until Jade didn't react fearfully at all to the sound of the appliance. If Jade had not approached, Lauri would have left the hairdryer on but stepped away until Jade was willing to come to her. Then she would have worked her way slowly toward the appliance, reinforcing Jade for each step closer.

The next noise project was another one of necessity. Jade was clearly fearful of any door that banged. She didn't even want to walk through doorways. This time Lauri put Jade on leash. Together they approached a closed door but stopped just short of the pup becoming fearful. Lauri gave her treats in that spot. Over the course of the first week, they went a bit closer during each session. Every time they stopped, there were plenty of treats. Finally they were close enough that Lauri could reach the door. She opened it slowly and treated Jade liberally. Then she closed it quietly and treated. Before the pup became anxious, they turned and left. Over the course of the week, they progressed from shutting the door with a tiny bang to slamming it shut. At the end of the week, she was excited to go through every door in the house.

Noise goblin number three also reared its head fairly quickly. The howling of the monster vacuum sent Jade into a huddle in her exercise pen. To work on this issue, Lauri recruited Richard to help. While Lauri took Jade outside to the patio, where she couldn't see the vacuum, Richard turned it on. Jade was relaxed enough to take treats, so

ew they were at the correct distance. Each session they moved a bit closer, but they did nto the same room for several days. Finally Jade would touch the vacuum when it was not In the end she could be in the room with it running.

hethodical work paid off. On their walks, Jade accepted noises such as the garage door with little reaction. If the pup found something that made noise and she initiated an on, Lauri gave Jade her favorite treat (Trader Joe's Italian meatballs).

he next months, Lauri continued to expose her pup to a variety of sounds. New issues hally came up, but each time, she followed a plan to desensitize the pup to the sound. The have been good. Each month, Jade's fears decreased, and by one year of age, she was ensitive to sound.

Don't lure or beg your puppy to approach something that makes him anxious—let him choose his response and reward him for being brave.

Process

1. Fill your pocket with treats. These can be part of your pup's regular food if he eats it happily. Leave the puppy loose in the vicinity as long as the area is enclosed.
2. Then simply fire up something noisy like your hairdryer. If the puppy walks up to you to investigate, praise him verbally and offer treats from your hand.
3. Repeat the game over several days. If introducing the first noise goes well, find another noise during your subsequent training sessions and repeat the exercise. Be creative. For example, the wall of a metal shed provides a perfect opportunity to make a banging noise, and a screaming teakettle on the stove is a great goblin.

During this work, it is very important that you don't lure or beg your puppy to approach something that makes him anxious. Let him choose his response and reward him when he is brave. Forcing your pup to come close to something fearful will damage your relationship with him.

If your pup will not approach a particular noise willingly, you need to move him farther away from the noisemaker. Take the pup just beyond the point where he is fearful. For example, if your dog is afraid of the garage door going up and down when you are 5 feet (1.5 m) away, move him back to 10 feet (3 m). If your pup is relaxed at that distance, start there. If not, move back even farther. Once you find the neutral spot, feed your pup while you raise and lower the door. The next day, repeat the exercise with your pup 1 foot (.5 m) closer. Deliver lots of treats one by one if your pup stays relaxed. You may

Trainer Talk

The process of gradually making a sound or situation less fear-producing is called "desensitization." Pups can be desensitized to sounds or anything in the environment that worries them. The steps in this section describe a classic desensitization process. Remember, you should never force a pup to approach something he is fearful about. If you try to help him get over a fear but don't see progress, it's beneficial to work with a training professional.

find that this is a good time to bring out your high-value treats so that your pup thinks this game is especially fun.

Over multiple sessions, move in toward the scary noise very slowly. Don't hurry. Always stay just beyond the point at which your pup becomes fearful.

Possible Challenges

Some dogs seem to have no issues with noises for months and then suddenly become fearful of a particular sound. Sometimes that sound can generalize to an entire setting. At about one year of age, my youngest Sheltie reacted strongly to the sound of a metal latch on a stall door being opened in a huge barn. Shortly after, we needed to walk through a different barn and he was distinctly anxious. Then he started to show fearfulness in any large covered building. Although he is a chowhound, he was so worried that he wouldn't even take a bit of food.

Using the process described here, I was able to desensitize him to barn-like settings and squeaky noises. We started outside the original barn at a "safe" distance. He was able to move closer to the barn only when he showed me that he was relaxed enough to take food from my hand. When we were able to take the final step back into the barn, we walked through quickly rather than hanging out so that he knew he wasn't trapped in there. Over time, we began to slow down until he could stand inside and relax.

Exercise #24: Off to Puppy Obedience Class

Goal: Continue to socialize your pup and practice your basic commands in a setting with lots of distractions.

Ideal Age to Start: 5 months

Groundwork: Find a good beginning obedience class before your pup is ready because many fill up quickly.

Clicker: Yes; use for practice in class with basic commands.

Background

If you and your pup enjoyed your kindergarten class, you may be lucky enough to slide right

Real-Life Pups

Starting at 8 weeks, future assistance dog pups attend obedience class weekly for 8 weeks and then every other week until they are 16 months. Pups love attending class. In fact, one of the challenges is not letting the pups drag their puppy raisers into the training room.

The trainer you choose should emphasize the importance of making training fun.

into your teacher's beginning obedience class. If that is not an option, most urban and suburban areas have dog clubs that offer public classes and private dog trainers who offer a variety of puppy options. If you are unfamiliar with classes in your area, try checking your newspaper's classified ads or look online for classes. Check the phone book, talk to dog friends, and even call your local humane society to make a list. When you have a list, talk with the teacher, and if possible, visit a class.

In selecting a class, I would suggest the following criteria for evaluating your teacher. She should:

- emphasize positive training (rather than correction-based training)
- encourage the use of clickers or marker words
- support a variety of tools, including the head halter or no-pull harness
- intervene in any situation in which a pup is fearful or confused
- have a variety of strategies to teach pups as individuals
- understand a pup's short attention span and switch activities often
- emphasize the importance of making training fun

Trainer Talk

Virtually anyone can set themselves up as a dog trainer. There are outstanding certified trainers and terrific noncertified teachers. Your best bet is to observe a potential class. If anything makes you uncomfortable when observing a class, trust your gut feeling and take your pup somewhere else. Once you are enrolled in a class, you can always sit out an activity that doesn't seem right for your pup.

Process

Attend your class regularly and do your homework. If your pup gets tired in class, just let him take a time-out and watch the other pups for a bit. It is never productive to try teaching a pup who is fatigued.

Possible Challenges

If you live outside a town, you may need to travel. This is a worthwhile activity unless you have friends with young dogs and can create your own beginning obedience class.

Chapter 10
Attention and
Self-Control

Exercise #25: Meet and Greet

Goal: Teach your pup to sit quietly by your side while you chat with a friend and to accept being petted by a friendly stranger.

Ideal Age to Start: 10 weeks

Groundwork: Your pup should have some experience with walking on the leash and the *sit* command. However, neither of these commands needs to be perfect in order to start this exercise.

Clicker: No

Background

Because you will want to take your pup out in public on many field trips, it is important that he learn good manners for interacting with all those folks who will want to pet him. Remember, it might seem innocent to let your little pup jump on people, but this behavior will not be charming when he is bigger.

Unlike other activities in this book, we are not teaching a new command here. All you are doing is teaching your dog to stay seated while someone touches him. Your only command will be *sit* with the expectation that your pup will learn over time to stay seated until released.

For a dog to go on field trips, he must learn to display good manners with all the people who will want to pet him.

Real-Life Pups

In the first photo you can see a pup starting to learn how to control himself as a person approaches. The handler is holding the pup's rear end. In the second and third photos you can see the final product. This lovely girl understands that her job is to sit even when a stranger gazes at her.

 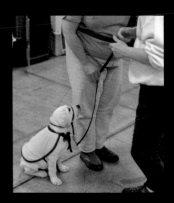 

This activity is part of the American Kennel Club's (AKC) Canine Good Citizen test for good reason. To pass this particular test, your pup or dog must first sit quietly while you exchange pleasantries with an evaluator. He must not be shy, lunge, or need forcible restraint. Next the pup must sit or stand quietly, without jumping, while the evaluator pets him. Just like real life, eh?

Pups react to this activity in very different ways. Lower-energy pups will learn to sit quietly with just a bit of coaching from you. Active pups and pups who just love, love, love people find it challenging to learn the self-control required to stay seated when faced with the prospect of a new friend. If you have one of these wiggle bunnies, read the possible challenges below.

During this exercise, remember what you learned in Love That Touch (Exercise #4) about how pups dislike having hands reaching for their heads. Inevitably, this is where people want to touch them. We find that with the assistance dog pups, if we ask people to pet them on the chest or shoulder, the pups are much happier and learn to relax while meeting new friends.

Process

Phase One
Ask a friend or two to help you with this exercise.
1. Have your pup sit. Grasp his collar and put your hand gently on his bottom (don't push) to keep him seated.
2. Ask your friend to approach, bend down, and scratch your pup quickly on the chest or shoulder.

Have her back up immediately.

3. Give your pup a treat from your bag while he continues to sit.
4. Release him to stand up by lifting him up gently.
5. Repeat over several sessions until you can tell that your pup doesn't need your hand on his rear end to stay seated.

Phase Two

1. Play the same game with your hand on your pup's collar only. Keep your eyes on him as your friend pets in case he pops up.
2. If he does, place your hand gently on his bottom to remind him to sit.
3. Each time he continues to sit for the petting, praise and reinforce while he is still seated. You may feed your pup very slowly during the petting to remind him that you are more interesting than anyone else.

If you plan to do the Canine Good

If your dog remains seated while being petted, praise him and reinforce the behavior with several treats.

Citizen test, have your friend start to mix in some head petting. In this program, the evaluator is instructed to pet both the pup's head and body. This is because the AKC recognizes that folks are likely to reach for your pup's noggin.

Phase Three

1. When your pup is sitting calmly for petting, remove your hand from his collar. Stand up straight now.
2. Feed him from your bag very slowly as he is petted so that his attention is on you rather than your friend.
3. As your friend approaches, shake hands and take a minute or two to chat. Have your friend ask, "May I pet your dog?" Then have her pet him on the head and body.
4. If he remains seated, praise him and reinforce his good behavior with several treats.

Practice this game regularly until your pup is at least a year old. Because it takes tremendous self-control on the pup's part, you must continue to reinforce it for many months.

Possible Challenges

Some young pups love people so much that they become whirling dervishes when a friend approaches. This behavior will only get wilder if you let it. Three hints. First, make sure to hold your pup's collar and bottom as described so that he learns that he can stay seated. Gradually, over time, you will be able to hold less and less. Second, try feeding your pup as he is petted. This will help him relax and stay seated. Gradually, you can feed less frequently as he understands his job. Third, ask folks to keep the petting short. The longer the petting episode, the more an excitable pup will wind himself higher and higher. This training session is better to set up with your friends because it is harder to control interactions with folks you don't know.

If your older pup gets immensely excited when another person approaches, you need a different approach. Have a friend stand some distance away and not look at your pup. Looking at your pup is an invitation to play. Approach your friend with your pup on leash and his head halter or no-pull harness. Before your pup gets excited, ask him to sit, click, and reward him. Then start forward, take only a step or two, and repeat I Can Sit (Exercise #10). Continue toward your friend to the point that your pup can control himself, but not beyond. Then end the session. During your next outing, approach your friend in the same way, sitting and rewarding your pup multiple times before he loses control. Try to get at least one step closer than you did last session, with your pup focused on you because you are clicking and rewarding. Resist the urge to tighten your leash because this will just excite him.

Each training session, work your pup one or two steps closer but never to the point that he turns into a wiggle machine. When the day comes that you are able to come within handshaking distance of your friend with your pup sitting quietly next to you, make sure that your partner keeps her eyes off the pup and folds her arms so that the pup can't lunge for a pet. Stay close just long enough to praise your pup and then turn and leave. During subsequent sessions, stay close to your friend longer and longer. Remember to praise and treat your pup while he maintains his self-control. Soon you will be able to shake hands with your friend and talk for a few moments before she pets your pup's chest or shoulder.

Trainer Talk

I find that one of the biggest things that separate experienced and novice trainers is the attention they pay to their pups during every training session. The experienced folks never let their attention waver. Their eyes stay on the pup when I am talking and when they are working their pup. This means that they catch and reinforce behaviors they like and stop their pups from doing things that they don't want. If you are a newer puppy teacher, strive to keep your eyes and attention on your pup from the time you get out of the car at class or on field trips right until you put your pup back in. Spacing out in class means that your pup will, at the least, wander off and start playing with other pups. Your goal is to work together.

Exercise #26: Watch Me

Goal: Teach your puppy to check in regularly by looking at your face.
Ideal Age to Start: 10 weeks
Groundwork: Frontload the Clicker (Exercise #2)
Clicker: Yes

Background

There is just nothing better than a dog who looks up at you adoringly when you are working together on training exercises or just hanging out. Some trainers try to get this behavior by teaching a formal *watch me* command. The problem is that this implies the dog should look up at you only when you give the command. Also, it is never clear when the dog is free to stop watching you.

   I prefer to have a dog who checks in regularly with me on his own. This is easy to teach if you simply reinforce your pup for frequently looking at your face. Remember, you will get whatever behaviors you reinforce.

Process

Phase One

1. Put your clicker in one hand and your leashed pup in the other.

Real-Life Pups

These three photos demonstrate pups at different stages of learning *watch me*. Baby Jade is playing the game in front of Lauri, who is holding a toy that Jade loves. Next is an adolescent Border Collie who has started to play the game in the *heel* position. The picnic bench is acting as a barrier to keep the pup in place. In the final photo, a year-old Canine Companion has learned this game to perfection. Note that the handler is perfectly quiet and the dog is choosing this eye contact.

2. Just stand quietly with your hands by your side. Don't say anything to your pup. Let your pup do whatever he wants.
3. The minute he glances in your direction, click and treat.
   Play the game for up to a minute.
Remember to work only on the single variable of eye contact. Play this game over several sessions until your pup glances at you every few seconds.

Phase Two
Expand the time that you play. Play for two minutes, clicking and treating each time your pup glances at you. Then make it three, four, and five minutes. By now, your pup should love looking at you. It is fine if he stares at you or if he chooses to glance back and forth between you and the environment. Either way, he is actively checking in with you.

Reinforce your pup for frequently looking at your face.

Phase Three
Now you will work on getting your pup to gaze at you over a period of time.
1. Click and treat when he glances at you as you have been doing.
2. If he keeps his eyes on you, click and treat again.
3. If he continues to look, you can click and reinforce every few seconds. Be careful not to click once your pup looks away because that will give him the wrong message.
   Once your pup is comfortable looking at you, you can click and reinforce less frequently. However, to maintain his eye contact, you should surprise him every now and then with your marker and a reward.

Phase Four
The final step is to teach your pup to glance at you from the *heel* position.
1. Sit your pup next to a barrier so that he can't flip in front of you.
2. Stand quietly and wait for him to look up: *Hey, when are we going to get going here*?
3. As he does, click and treat while he remains at your side. He will understand quickly that this is the same game you have been playing with just a change of location.
   Over time, you can work on lengthening the time that he looks at you while walking at your side.

Possible Challenges
If by chance your dog is more interested in looking at something else rather than at you, change your location to somewhere less stimulating. Once you find the place where you are more

Trainer Talk

Trainers think in terms of "variables." A variable is something, such as a behavior, that you can change. The variable in this game is the eye glance from the pup.

Variables are an important concept in puppy training because pups get confused if you tell them you like two different behaviors in one lesson. For example, imagine that you are planning to teach your dog to speak on command at a later date. When you then switch to teaching your pup this *watch me* game, your pup may bark because he wants to get the treat. If you switch the game back and give him a treat for speaking, he will become very confused about what you are asking him to do. Rather, you should ignore the bark and wait for the eye glance that you are trying to teach. Then mark and reinforce that. If the pup were to look at you and bark simultaneously, you cannot reward either, because the pup will have no idea which behavior you liked.

Before any lesson, think about what variable you are working on. Any time your pup appears confused, stop for a minute and consider whether you may be trying to teach too many things at once.

interesting than the environment, practice there for several days. Then very gradually play the game in places with more distractions. If at any time your pup is unable to check in with you, find a quieter place for a review.

Sometimes in my class, I notice that handlers fall into the habit of begging their dog to pay attention. They will tap their dog on the head or say the pup's name repeatedly. Inevitably, these dogs continue to look away. At the risk of imposing my human emotions, the dogs who are getting nagged often look embarrassed to me. The bottom line is that it is your pup's job to offer his attention, not for you to nag to get it. You can achieve that by playing this game.

Exercise #27: Hurry

Goal: Teach your pup to potty on command.
Ideal Age to Start: 5 months
Groundwork: Housetraining on Steroids (Exercise #8)
Clicker: No

Background

This is very useful when you are trying to leave the house and need to get your pup to go. Pups who really understand this command will actually go out and try to go even if they don't really have to.

We are going to skip the clicker with this command because pups often get so excited hearing the click that they stop piddling. Just use praise and cookies.

Process

Phase One
1. Simply watch for your pup to piddle.
2. As soon as he is finishing, say the command "hurry."
3. When he is done, praise your pup and give him a treat.
4. Repeat this 30 to 50 times.

Phase Two
Repeat the same exercise except start using your *hurry* command while your pup is going.

Phase Three
1. Next, when you can tell your pup is going to go for sure, give your command *hurry*.
2. Repeat this for a couple of months. This is longer than we usually stay at this stage, but we want the pup to really understand the connection between the word and his bodily functions.

Real-Life Pups

Although I had taught *hurry* in classes for years, I had never taught it to my own dogs until I added my youngest Sheltie, Boo. I followed this game exactly as described. Now when we go outside and I use the command, he races over to a bush and lifts his leg, even if nothing happens. He looks at me as if to say, *See, I told you*. Although he is now two and a half, I still reward him with a piece of toasted oat cereal now and then to keep him trying.

The *hurry* cue is useful when you are trying to leave the house and need to get your pup to go on command.

Phase Four
Now we're ready for the big test. Give the command when you need your pup to go. You can tell when he really knows this drill because he will go try even if he doesn't need to when you give the command. Remember not to do this if there is any question in your mind whether he will go. If he doesn't go, return to the previous step for a week or two.

Phase Five
1. Gradually use your command in increasingly distracting settings. In each new location, you should feel fairly certain that he would go before you say "Hurry."
2. Each time he responds in a new place, reinforce profusely with cookies.

Trainer Talk
The tone of voice that you use to praise or encourage your pup matters. A higher, happy voice is very motivational to dogs. A low voice slows dogs down. One of the most amusing aspects of training classes is teaching guys to raise their voices when they talk to their pups. You can prove this to yourself by speaking to your pup in a higher octave than you normally use while you practice heeling. You will notice that your pup starts prancing when you find a tone that he likes. When you are working on the *hurry* command, praise your pup in a tone of voice that leaves no doubt in his mind that you are pleased with him.

Possible Challenges
Be cautious not to give the command too early in this game. If you give the command and the dog doesn't go, you are teaching him to ignore your request. For several months, you need to time your word so that you have 100 percent success.

Exercise #28: Wait Right There
Goal: When working on leash, teach your dog to stop next to you on command and wait until released or given another command.
Ideal Age to Start: 6 months
Groundwork: Your dog should be working on the Casual *Heel* (Exercise #14).
Clicker: Yes

Background
There are many times when it is useful to have your pup stop, stand quietly, and wait until you say that it is okay to move forward. You can use this command at a curb while you check traffic. You can put it into action when you need to pick up dropped keys. You can use it while you gather an armful of packages.

Puppy raisers often ask the difference between *wait* and *stay* (see Exercise #16: Stay!). The *wait* command is less formal. It simply means that your forward momentum has stopped for a moment. It is like hitting pause on the television—the pup simply stops next to you. It doesn't matter if he stands or sits down as long as there is no pulling. *Stay* is a more formal command. It means that the pup is put in a position such as a *sit* and should stay there until you return and tell him what to do next.

Process

Phase One

1. The first step in teaching this command is to show your pup that there are times he will need to stop walking. Ask him to walk forward next to you using your *heel* command. Your leash should be loose as we discussed in the Casual *Heel* (Exercise #14).
2. Without saying anything, tighten your leash just a bit to make your pup slow down, and rotate quickly in front of him. You will end up facing your pup. If he continues walking, he will bump into you. You will know if you are turning too slowly because your dog will be able to walk past you. Put on those dancing shoes and pick up your speed.
3. As soon as you are in front of your pup, click and offer him a treat.
4. To start moving forward, simply rotate back next to your pup and start walking again.
5. Go a few feet (m) and rotate in front of him again. Practice this move over several sessions.

After just a couple of lessons at home, you can start rotating in front of your pup anyplace you will want him to wait regularly. This will help him develop the habit of stopping and waiting for your direction. Once your pup starts to slow up or stops when he sees you turning in front of him, you are ready for the next level.

Phase Two

1. Add your command *wait* once you are in front of your pup.
2. Click and reinforce.

Phase Three

1. When your pup no longer needs you to pull back on the leash, begin saying your *wait* command while you are turning in front of him.
2. Continue to click and reinforce after you have rotated to face him.

The *wait* command teaches your dog to stop next to you on command and wait until released or given another command.

Phase Four

Your pup will start slowing up on his own when he sees you start to rotate. That is an indication that it's time to eliminate the rotation. To help your pup remember to stop, you are going to use a hand cue like a stop sign.

1. Start with your *heel* command.
2. When you want your pup to wait, just swing your right hand across your body and use it like a stop sign in front of his face. This motion should not be so fast as to scare the pup. Most pups respond very quickly to this hand motion and stop on a dime.
3. Give the verbal *wait* command as you bring your hand across.

Phase Five

Give your verbal command before you cue your dog with your hand. Remember that the *wait* should be followed *after a few seconds* with another command such as *heel*.

Phase Six

Now it's time to let your pup take responsibility for stopping.

1. Walk up to a curb or location where you have practiced many times.
2. Give your *wait* command with no hand cue.

Real-Life Pups

These three photos show several levels of development. In the first, the handler is rotating in front of the pup so that the pup has to stop. In the second, the handler is using her arm like a stop sign to cue the pup to stop. In the final photo, you see an older pup who understands her job and is waiting at a doorway until she hears her next command.

3. If your pup stops next to you without tightening the leash, mark the behavior and treat, treat, treat. Don't move forward until you give your next command.

Phase Seven
Start using your command at different locations. For example, if you take your pup on play dates, have him wait at the gate to the play area rather than just going wild. Then use your *release* command to free him to play.

Possible Challenges
Your goal is to teach your pup to take responsibility for stopping when you ask him to wait. If your pup has learned his job, the leash will remain loose as you and the pup stop moving.

It is useful to watch your leash as you stop. If your pup tightens the leash at all, he is letting you manage his behavior rather than demonstrating self-control. In that case, surprise him regularly by rotating in front of him or using your hand as a stop sign. Make this a lively game so that he never knows when you are going to help him with an arm cue or when he is responsible. When he does stop on his own, click and throw a party.

Exercise #29: It Pays to Come
Goal: Teach your dog to come even when faced with a tempting distraction.
Ideal Age to Start: 8 months (or earlier if your pup is not coming consistently)
Groundwork: Play the *recall* games you have learned in Chapters 7 and 8.
Clicker: No

Background
One of the most frequent things puppy raisers say to me is that their pups come when called… except when there is something more interesting in the vicinity, such as another dog or a possible treat. For the command to be useful and to keep your dog safe, you need to be able to call him to you even when there is something exciting to investigate. This is very possible, with practice, if you convince your pup that the payoff from you is always better than the payoff from the environment.

The following is a controlled game that you can play to guarantee that your pup will be successful. It does take two, so recruit a partner and play it for a few minutes every day. If you

To keep your dog safe, you need to be able to call him to you at all times.

Trainer Talk

One thing to remember is that dogs have relatively poor vision. Dog eye doctors suggest that pups can clearly see about 20 feet (6 m) compared to our 80 feet (24.5 m). Add the fact that they see only limited colors and it is clear that their world looks very different from ours. Their eyes definitely come in a distant third to their powerful noses and ears.

When you are playing games like It Pays to Come with your pup, it is possible that he simply can't see you once you walk away. You can help him by not going quite as far until he learns to look for you. A second strategy is to back up slowly while he looks for you. Pups can find moving objects more easily than stationary objects.

start to lose interest in working on your pup's *recall*, think of the following scenario: Your dog slips out the door and races toward a busy street. You call him. He turns and races back to you joyously. Whew.

For this game you will use an expanding leash or long line. Check that it is the appropriate weight for your pup. A leash that is too heavy will prevent a small puppy from moving forward as you will be asking him to do.

Process

Phase One

You might start this in your yard, but a parking lot or even a quiet street works well.

1. Give your partner a handful of low-value treats. Put your pup on your expandable leash. Have your partner hold it. Make sure that the leash is not in locked position.
2. Show your pup a high-value treat, like a bit of hot dog.
3. Turn and run away. If you are teaching a younger pup, don't go more than 10 feet (3 m) away. For an older pup, 15 to 20 feet (4.5 to 6 m) is fine. While you are moving away, your partner should show the pup a treat but not allow him to eat it. This distracts the pup from you.
4. As soon as you get to your spot, turn around and call your pup. Use a very happy, encouraging voice. As you call, your friend should move her treat behind her back so that the pup doesn't obsess about it.
5. As soon as the pup locks in on you, continue to call and back up a few steps.
6. Once the pup starts to move toward you, the holder should let the leash expand and hang behind the pup. This way the pup is focused on you and not the person running next to him.

7. When your pup arrives in front of you, feed him tiny bits of cookie for at least 15 seconds.

Phase Two
Gradually move a bit farther back each time you call your pup. Remember to throw a party when he arrives.

Phase Three
Stop showing your pup a treat before you run away, and don't take your treats out until he arrives. This is important because he may learn to come only when you have a treat in your hand. When he arrives, dole the treats out of your bag generously. Tell him what a fine, fine puppy he is.

Phase Four
Now you will make the game even harder. Have your friend continue to hold the treat in front of your pup's nose while you call. Remember, this is not a high-value treat. Your pup should realize that coming to you and your hot dog bits (which are in your bag until he arrives) is a much better deal.

Phase Five
Change the game so that your puppy holder also has a high-value treat. By now, your pup should know that his job is to ignore that cookie in order to get to you.

Real-Life Pups
Here is a pup playing the come exercise. In the first photo, the puppy holder is distracting him with a low-value treat while the handler runs away. In the second photo, the holder hangs back while the handler encourages the pup and then rewards the pup for coming when called. In the third photo, note the young terrier's enthusiasm for getting to his handler when called.

Phase Six

Move the same game to a new location with more stimulation. I take my pup and my friend to a neighborhood park with joggers. When this goes well, I increase the challenge again by taking him to another park with a softball game and kids thundering around the bases. Play in as many places as you can think of. Each time your pup chooses you, reward him generously.

Possible Challenges

Occasionally pups stall out and don't move toward the puppy raiser. This happens for one of two reasons.

1. Pups who are a bit timid or super compliant seem to feel that they are supposed to stay where they are left. If your pup is reluctant to move forward, have your puppy holder walk forward a bit with the pup and then hold back once he realizes that it is okay to move. Recently I worked with a young Lab cross who never takes chances. It took three repetitions with lots of treats for her to realize that it was okay to travel between holder and puppy raiser.

2. A second reason for a pup to stall out is that he simply loses track of you. A pup's vision is not great. For your young pup, stay close enough in the beginning so that he can find you. After playing the game a few times, he will learn to look for you. If he gets confused, come closer and then gradually increase the distance.

Exercise #30: Bed

Goal: Teach your dog to go to his bed when asked and stay there until released.
Ideal Age to Start: 9 months
Groundwork: Your pup should be familiar with two commands. First, he should be comfortable with the *down* command. Although you won't be using this command specifically, you will be luring your pup into a *down* as part of this new game. In addition, your pup should be confident with *stay* while you move to the end of your leash for a minute or two.
Clicker: Yes

Background

When you teach this command, you will be able to send your pup to a designated spot to relax until you are done eating or completing a task. When this is taught well and reinforced consistently, you can prevent begging at the table but keep your eye on your teenager.

`You will notice that teaching this command is exactly the same as teaching *under* (see

Trainer Talk

Remember that you must be careful what you reinforce. If your pup gets up during the *bed* exercise or others like it and you give him a treat to get him back in position, you have effectively rewarded him for getting up.

The *bed* command sends your pup to a designated spot to relax until you are done eating or completing a task.

Exercise #31: Under) except there is a bed involved rather than a desk or table.

Process

Phase One
1. Put your pup on leash. Place him on your left side and a treat in your right hand.
2. Show your pup the treat. Then lure him toward the bed.
3. Once the pup has walked onto the bed, use your treat to lure him into a *down*. I like to pull the lure toward me so that the pup turns to face me, but this is optional.
4. Lower the lure to the ground and hold it there until your pup lies down.
5. As soon as he settles down, click and mark the behavior and treat your pup. Immediately release him to get up and off the bed.

Phase Two
Repeat the same game, but do it without a food lure in your hand at least half the time. Do continue to cue your dog with your hand.

1. As soon as your pup lies down on the bed, click or mark and treat liberally.
2. Start using your *bed* command after your pup has completed lying down.
3. Begin to extend the duration of the *bed* by feeding your pup very slowly as he remains down.

Phase Three

Keep playing the game, but drop the lure altogether. Continue to use your hand to cue your pup by drawing the path that you want him to travel. Remember to click or mark every time your pup lies down on the bed.

1. Start using your command just as your pup starts moving toward the bed.
2. Continue to extend the period of time your pup stays on the bed. Feed him just quickly enough that he wants to stay in the correct position. You may use your *stay* command to reinforce the idea that you want him to stay where he is.

   If your pup is getting confident with the game and is unlikely to take off for a run, you can start playing without the leash.

Phase Four

Once you are sure your pup will move forward, start using your command to initiate the performance.

Real-Life Pups

The pup in this first photo is at Phase One of the *bed* exercise. The pup in the second photo has learned to walk to his bed and lie down.

Phase Five
At this level, fade the cue with your hand.

Phase Six
Now you can work on moving away from the bed while your pup stays down. I find it works well to put the bed 2 or 3 feet (.5 or 1 m) from my sofa. I have the pup go to the bed and ask him to stay. I move to the sofa and sit down. On days that my aim is good, I toss treats on the bed just fast enough to encourage the pup to stay. After a couple of minutes, or as long as your pup can be successful, stand up, walk to the bed, treat your pup while he is lying down, and release him.

Trainer Talk
Teaching your pup new games and commands is just the first half of training. The second half is helping your pup maintain what he has learned. The best way to do this is to use your commands in daily life. For example, you might have your pup wait each time you go through the door to the car and each time you go to the backyard. Meals are a great time to practice

If your pup gets up and walks to you, gently return him to the bed. Don't give him a treat for lying back down or you will teach him that it is rewarding to get up.

Over the next few weeks, work on two variables. Alternate moving your pup's bed farther away from you and extending the time that you ask him to remain on the bed. Remember that if he is not successful at any time, you are asking too much too fast.

Possible Challenges
All pups can learn this command if you invest the training time. The only challenge is remembering to pay attention to your pup. It is easy to forget that he is on a command and must be released to get up. If you allow him to wander off when he chooses, he will lose his understanding that he is to stay on the bed.

Chapter 11
Just for Fun

Exercise #31: Under

Goal: Teach your dog to lie down under your desk or table while you work.

Ideal Age to Start: 7 months

Groundwork: Your pup should have experience with the *down* command.

Clicker: Yes

Background

This is a command that all future assistance dogs learn. It is great for using in restaurants, but you can also teach your pup to dive under your desk for a nap when you settle down to work at the computer.

The *under* command teaches a pup to walk completely under a table or desk and stay there.

The *under* command means that your pup walks completely under a table or desk, turns around to face you, and then lies down with no body parts sticking out to trip you. Initially your pup will learn to get under a piece of furniture. Then you will work on extending the period of time he remains there. If you are an overachiever, you might want to teach him to crawl under a low object such as a park bench.

Process

Phase One

1. Find a table or desk under which you would like your pup to lie. Take a pillow for you to kneel on.
2. Put your pup on leash, and place him on your left side with a treat in your right hand.
3. Show your pup the treat, then lure him under the table. Lean as far as you have to in order to get your pup completely under the table.
4. Slowly pull the lure toward you so that the pup turns to face you.
5. Lower the lure to the ground and hold it there until your pup lies down.
6. As soon as he settles down, click and mark the behavior and treat him. Immediately release him to come out from under the table.

Phase Two

After approximately 30 repetitions, it's time to fade the use of the food lure.

1. Cue your dog using your hand in the same sweeping motion under the table. I often describe the movement as drawing a big upside-down U.
2. As soon as your pup lies down under the table, click or mark and treat liberally. Alternate luring your pup with food to keep him interested in the game.

   During this phase, start using your *under* command after your pup has completed the *down*. Keep dropping your hand to the ground to help your pup understand that lying down is part of the game.

   Start to extend the duration of the *under* by feeding your pup very slowly as he remains down.

Phase Three

Keep playing the game, but drop the lure altogether.

1. Continue to use your hand to cue your pup by drawing the path that you want him to travel. Remember to click or mark every time your pup dives under, turns around, and lies down. Start using your command just as your pup starts turning to face you under the furniture.
2. Continue to extend the period of time your pup holds the *under*. Feed him just quickly enough that he wants to stay in the correct position.
3. When your pup is staying under for a couple of minutes, start transitioning from kneeling to standing up. When your pup is under, stand up. Bend over only to feed at intervals, to show him that you want him to stay down.

Phase Four

Start to use your command while your pup begins to move under the table.

Real-Life Pups

In these photos, you see a seven-month-old pup following a lure under a tall desk. Then, in the second photo, the handler is reinforcing the pup at intervals to encourage him to hold the position. In the final photo, the pup has learned to scoot under a much lower bench with just a couple of weeks of practice.

Phase Five

Once you are sure that your pup will move forward, start using your command to initiate the *under*.

Phase Six

At this level, you want to fade your use of the hand cue. You can do this by very gradually shortening the path that you draw. For example, draw only seven-eighths of the upside-down U. Reward generously every time your pup gets the behavior right with less help from you. Then draw three-quarters of the U. Then draw one-half. Continue until you can just flick your finger. Then fade that too. If at any point your dog gets less enthusiastic about diving under the table, extend your hand motion a bit.

Phase Seven

Initiate the behavior while you are standing. When your pup races under the table and lies down, reward him with lots of little cookies.

Possible Challenges

Sometimes handlers don't get their arm far enough back under the table. Then when the pup turns around and lies down, he is not under anything. Make sure to reach way

The *under* cue is useful because your dog can relax in a safe space while you work.

Trainer Talk

"Duration" refers to the length of time a pup continues a behavior. For example, when a pup is learning to lie down, it is reasonable to expect duration of a couple of seconds. Over time your pup can learn much longer duration for lying down. In fact, when he is a year old, a half hour or more is reasonable. In the same way, you can teach your puppy duration with the *under* command.

Novice trainers sometimes confuse teaching a command with teaching duration. Learning to sit and learning to stay seated are two completely different things. Duration is taught by rewarding the pup steadily while he holds a position as long as you desire. Remember to release your pup when you are ready to end any command.

back so that your pup has room to turn around. Obviously, tiny dogs require less reach than a Mastiff puppy.

Exercise #32: Find the Cookie (or Toy)

Goal: Teach your puppy to search for a hidden item.
Ideal Age to Start: 8 months
Groundwork: The puppy must have a passion for either food or a toy.
Clicker: No

Background

When I first introduced this game to the pack, I would hide a chunk of dog cookie behind the sofa or under a pillow or in a box and let all of the dogs search madly. The dog who found it got an immediate reward. One thing I learned quickly is that this is a game best played with one dog at a time unless you have two dogs closely matched in speed and neither is prone to food guarding. With my crew, one dog quickly came to dominate the game and the others were merely frustrated.

As a result, I began putting three-quarters of the pack in the bedroom and playing with the fourth individually. The dogs locked in the bedroom get some good exercise too since they are excited waiting their turn, and they are likely to start playing. Everyone gets a rotation into the game.

Dogs of any age and size who love food can learn to search enthusiastically for

Real-Life Pups

Some pups move through the steps in Find the Cookie very quickly because they find the game just pure fun. Here is a photo showing one of my dogs getting reinforced for having found a cookie in a cardboard box.

Dogs of any age and size who love food can learn to search enthusiastically for a reward that you have stashed somewhere.

a reward that you have stashed somewhere. Once your dog finds the cookie, you can reinforce the game by offering a few extra bits of food right where he found the first cookie. This is called rewarding at the source. This game is best played in the house.

Different breeds play this game with different styles. My dogs, who have no interest in digging, like finding the prize behind things, but if I put it under something such as a towel, they are baffled and just lay down nearby. On the other hand, some breeds naturally love to dig. A friend's Miniature Dachshund will dive into a loaded laundry basket to ferret out a hidden cookie.

Process

Phase One
Decide what your dog would like to find most. This can be a piece of food or a beloved toy. For the game to work, your dog must really want the item. It also needs to be big enough for the dog to find readily.

1. Hold your dog by the collar and let him watch you drop the cookie (substitute toy here if that lights up your pup) behind something such as a sofa.

2. Walk him back a few feet (m) and quickly release him. It is important to hold your dog's collar as you move him away from the cookie because this will get him excited.
3. If he wants the cookie, he will immediately run out and eat it. Remember, there is no need to talk, and you don't have to use your clicker for this game because the dog automatically gets a reward for locating the hidden prize.
4. Repeat this step but move your dog back 1 or 2 feet (.3 or .6 m) farther away from the cookie. If he is having as much fun as most do, you can migrate back fairly quickly. Keep dropping the treat behind the same object for the first day or two.

Phase Two
For the next few days, play the same game, but each day put the cookie behind a different piece of furniture. Make sure it is easy to find the cookie. For each repetition, move your dog back a bit farther. During any one session, don't switch hiding places. Use your *find it* command after your pup has just located the prize. By saying the command after the dog has already found the cookie, you guarantee he will hear it after he has been successful.

Phase Three
Once your dog clearly understands this game, start adding a verbal command, like "Find it!" while he is running to get the cookie.

Phase Four
When your dog can easily run from across the room to find the cookie, it's time to make the game a bit harder.

1. Start alternating the places you "hide" the cookie during the same session. Begin by using two places that you have been putting the prize. Your dog is still watching you drop the cookie but now has to think where to go when you release him. Sometimes he will run to the place where he found the last cookie first. Just relax and let him find it on his own.
2. When this goes well, start moving the cookie to one of three different places in the same vicinity. For example, I use two sofas and a spot behind my desk.
3. When your dog is actively searching in several locations, you can start using your *find it* command before you release him.

Your dog's incredible sense of smell will help him locate the object you've hidden.

Phase Five

Once your pup persists and finds the cookie in multiple locations, it is time to up the ante.
1. Take him out of the room and shut the door.
2. Hide the cookie but in a very obvious place. It may even be easily seen the first time. Give your *find it* command, and immediately release your dog.

Phase Six

Continue to play the game described in the last step, but gradually make the hiding place more and more difficult. For example, you might put the cookie behind an entirely new piece of furniture.

Possible Challenges

Occasionally the human half of the team gets excited about this game and gives the dog a challenge that is just too difficult for his level of understanding. If at any time your dog is unable to be successful, simplify the game again for him and add challenges more slowly.

For example, if you have taught your pup to search for the treat on the floor, there is a good chance that he will not find a treat that you have hidden under a pillow on the sofa. You can fix this by starting at Phase One and teaching him that some prizes might be hidden in a new type of location. Gradually you can add the new spot into his repertoire. The more the dog plays, the more you will see his ability to think about possible hiding places.

Exercise #33: Hide-and-Seek

Goal: In this slightly adapted version of the children's game, you will teach your pup to look for you after you have hidden in the house.

Real-Life Pups

Here is a photo of my pack waiting to come and look for me. This photo was snapped just before I took off for a hiding spot in the far corner of the upstairs. On nice days, we leave the sliding door open so the game can include hiding places inside and outside the house.

Ideal Age to Start: 7 months
Groundwork: No
Clicker: No

Background

This game is good for puppies for at least two reasons. First, it teaches your pup how to look for you if you lose sight of each other. Developing that desire to search for you is definitely a relationship builder. Second, it is a great way to wear your pup out on a rainy day.

This game requires a partner to play. Your partner will restrain your pup while you hide.

Don't use your *stay* or *wait* commands in this game because you want the pup eager to look for you.

The game will start with very simple hiding places. By the time your pup has played a few times, you will be wracking your brain for nooks and crannies that will challenge him.

Process

Phase One

1. Fill your pocket with small delectable treats.
2. Have your partner grasp the pup gently by his buckle collar, and show the pup a treat.
3. Run away but not very far. Just duck around a corner out of sight.
4. Your partner should release the pup. He will, of course, chase you.
5. As soon as he locates you, praise and treat him. Be careful that you don't crouch and spring up when your pup comes around the corner, because this can seriously startle him and make him less enthusiastic to play.

Hide-and-seek teaches your pup to look for you after you have hidden in the house.

Trainer Talk

You have likely heard about dogs' incredible sense of smell. It is estimated to be 1 to 10,000 times as powerful as ours. Dog trainers and medical professionals are teaming up to put this magical snout to work sniffing out cancer.

If you are fascinated with your pup's ability to capture scents on the ground and in the air, you may enjoy getting involved in the sport of tracking. In this organized activity, dogs are trained to follow tracks that have been laid for them. Dogs of every size can participate in tracking. Several years ago, a tiny Papillon wowed the dog world by winning a national tracking championship in rough terrain during terrible weather conditions. You will find more information about dog sports toward the end of this book.

Your pup's confidence will grow in leaps and bounds each time he finds you.

6. Walk your pup back to your partner, telling him what a great pup he is the whole way.
7. Have the partner grasp the collar again. Again show the treat and then run. Hide in a new place but still quite close to the pup. Celebrate when he finds you.

Phase Two

When your pup finds you easily and consistently, add a bit of distance. Don't make your hiding place too hard, though. I find that ducking behind a door is enough of a challenge at this level. In our house, my partner holds the pup at the bottom of the stairs. I run up and into a bedroom where I duck behind the door. Again, I am very cautious not to startle the pup when he finds me.

In most cases, resist the urge to help your pup while he is looking for you. You'll notice that most pups tend to return to the spot you were previously before they start looking around. Give your pup time to think. If you can tell he is lost, whisper his name once or twice quietly. He will find you.

Your pup's confidence will grow in leaps and bounds if he is successful. He will be thrilled each time he finds you.

Phase Three

Now you can start to get a little more creative about hiding. I crouch down behind the bed or get under a desk. Since the pup still sees the direction I am running, he can handle the challenge.

Phase Four

Have your partner turn the pup around so that he doesn't actually see you leave. Initially hide in places similar to those in Phase Three. When your pup reliably finds you in familiar places, you can get serious about hiding. At this level, I crouch in the back of a dark walk-in closet or hide in the tub behind the curtain. Remember to continue rewarding your pup each time he finds you.

You can also take this game outside if you can find a fenced area with hiding places. Trees provide great cover.

Possible Challenges

If at any time your pup's enthusiasm for finding you wanes, you have gone too far too fast. Hide in more obvious places for a bit and be very generous with your treats when he finds you.

Exercise #34: Stand Up

Goal: Teach your puppy to go from a *sit* to a *stand.*
Ideal Age to Start: 7 months
Groundwork: I Can Sit (Exercise #10)
Clicker: Yes

Background

Teaching a dog to pop into a standing position from a *sit* and remain standing until asked to do something else is a traditional obedience exercise. I find it very useful for grooming, veterinary visits, and generally wowing my friends.

The *stand* command means that a dog gets up but doesn't walk around. Your pup should also stand up when you use your *release* command, but with that command, he is then free to wander close by or even lie down. The process described below gets the pup to stand up with minimal physical contact and also keeps him from wandering off.

Trainer Talk

My motto is: A tired pup is a good pup. Exercising your dog's body should be part of your daily routine. For a toy dog, a ball game in the hallway for 15 minutes may do the trick. For a larger dog, a walk around the block or even for a mile (1.5 km) is just a warm-up. This is particularly true now that your dog is not expending as much energy growing. Dogs need to run regularly. When the weather is bad, exercise is an interesting challenge. Find the Cookie (or Toy) (Exercise #32) and Hide-and-Seek (Exercise #33) are favorites in our house.

Process

Phase One

1. Have your puppy sit right in front of you. Make sure to click and reward that behavior. When you start doing two commands in a row, it is tempting to ignore the first command. If you do that, the pup will quickly learn the routine and just leap to the second command. And some folks think dogs aren't smart!

2. Shorten your leash just enough that your pup can't back up.

3. Without saying anything, take one step directly toward your pup. Because pups don't want anyone to step on their paws, they will automatically stand up. With a pup who likes to sit, you may need to step directly between his paws before he pops up.

The *stand* command will make it easier for you to groom your dog.

4. When the pup is on his feet, hesitate for just a second or two, then click and reinforce with a treat. *Hey,* you might be saying. *That is not what you said before. You told me to always time my click exactly with the behavior.* That was true, but on more complex commands like the *stand,* it doesn't always work. In this case, your dog may stand and then sit back down. If you move too quickly, you will mark the *sit* rather than the *stand,* which is counterproductive. To prevent this, just wait a couple of seconds to make sure that your dog is standing solidly. Then click and treat.

Remember, no words. Let your clicker do the talking. Because your dog is used to the clicker now, he will understand that whenever you click, you like what he is doing.

Phase Two

After a few practice sessions and when your pup shows he is very comfortable with this transition from *sit* to *stand,* start to give your *stand* command while your pup is on the way up.

Phase Three

Next, wean the pup from your body cue.

1. Gradually start to shorten your step toward the dog.

2. Each time he stands, pause slightly, click, and throw a small treat party.

Phase Four
When your pup stands with just a tiny foot movement, start using the verbal command to initiate the behavior. Your sequence should be the following:
1. Say your verbal command.
2. Take a small step toward your pup.
3. Pause and then click if your pup is clearly standing.
4. Pause and reinforce with a cookie.

Phase Five
Your goal now is to eliminate all foot movement. Cut down the length of your step systematically over several training sessions. In trainer lingo, this is called "fading the cue." The day will come when you stand still, use your verbal command, and watch your pup leap to his feet. To maintain the new behavior, make sure to continue to click and treat.

Real-Life Pups
For this exercise, the pictures say it best. The first photo shows Lauri rewarding Jade for sitting. Because Lauri wanted her pup to be eager to perform both the *stand* and *sit*, she still consistently rewarded the *sit*. In the next photo, you see Jade standing as Lauri steps toward her. Despite that raised paw, Lauri never touched her feet. Look at that tongue anticipating a food reward. The third photograph shows Jade beginning to stand before Lauri's foot actually comes forward. The puppy is already reading the bent knee as a signal to stand up. This demonstrates that the pup is ready to have the body cue faded. Lauri gradually shortened her step and eventually needed no foot movement for Jade to respond.

Trainer Talk

Trainers often talk about "fading the cue." This is the process of weaning the puppy from some motion you have been using to help your pup during the learning process. For example, when teaching *stand,* you cue your pup by stepping forward.

The fading process simply means that you gradually move less and less as your dog performs the behavior. In this case your step forward becomes shorter and shorter. When you taught *under,* the sweeping hand motion you used to cue your dog gradually became shorter and shorter until your puppy no longer needed it.

Possible Challenges

There are three things that you might encounter when playing this game, none of them serious. First, some pups who have done a lot of *sit* practice may stand up but then plop right back down. You need to help your pup understand that you like the *stand* as much as you like the *sit.* To accomplish this, have your pup stand a couple of times as described, then immediately reach out and tickle his belly while he is on all four feet. No need to click on these repetitions because he is already getting rewarded with petting. Then do the exercise again without the tummy tickle, and if he remains up, click and treat, treat, treat. It is good to delay your click for a few seconds to make sure that he is solid on standing.

Another related challenge is that some pups will try to scoot back while in a seated position when you step into them. If you encounter this with your pup, shorten your leash and take a bigger step toward him. Unable to move back, most dogs quickly jump up and you can mark and reward the behavior.

Third, an occasional dog will jump on the handler as she moves toward him. If this is an issue, try an alternative method. Put your pup at your side. Step forward with your foot closest to the pup. The pup will stand because he thinks you are leaving. Then bring the hand farthest from the pup across your body like a stop sign. (You did this earlier with the *wait* command.) This motion stops the dog from continuing to move forward.

Exercise #35: Where's John?

Goal: Teach your pup to recognize names and go to the correct person when sent.
Ideal Age to Start: 9 months
Groundwork: Hide-and-Seek (Exercise #33) is a good preliminary game because it teaches your pup to go and look for someone.
Clicker: No

Background

This game just expands Hide-and-Seek (Exercise #33) by asking your pup to distinguish among people by name and go to the correct person. It will initially require three people to play, and you can gradually expand the game to a full house. You are going to use food in a cup as a noisemaker to guarantee that your pup selects the correct person.

Process

Phase One
Give your two friends a supply of treats in something that can be shaken to make noise. Paper cups are perfect.

1. Start by having one friend shake her cup and give the pup a treat so that the sound acquires a positive association. Then have the other friend do the same. Continue until the pup understands that the sounds mean a good treat will follow.
2. Once your pup is excited by the sounds of the food in the cup, position both friends about 10 feet (3 m) from you but in plain sight. Hold your pup until your friends are ready.
3. Have one person shake her cup, and release your pup.
4. When he runs up to the correct person with the cup, have her praise him and give him several treats. If the pup runs to the other person, have her just remain silent.
5. After your pup finishes eating his treats, go get him and lead him back to the starting place.
6. Repeat the same game with the same person. Don't worry about names or commands at this point. After five trips to one person, switch people.

   Continue to play this game for several days. Don't increase the distance between you and your friends just yet.

Phase Two
1. Play the same game but with one adjustment: Start using your command after your pup arrives at the correct person. This will be the word "Where's" and the correct name of the person, such as "Where's John?"
2. Repeat this exercise with the same person at least five times. Then switch and play the game having your pup go to the other person. Naturally, you will change your command to reflect the new name. If the names are very similar and hard for a dog to discriminate, you might give one friend a distinctive nickname.

Phase Three
Again, make just one change. After your

Real-Life Pups

One of my Papillons was brilliant at Where's John? He originally learned the members of the family as described here. We even used the game to send him back and forth on the beach when we were widely separated. Later he could very quickly add a guest to the list of names he understood. I would say the guest's name a few times and have the guest reward him with a cookie for coming. After that, he could include them as if they were a family member. This game was an incredible crowd pleaser.

friend shakes the cup and while your pup is on his way to your friend, with no chance of making a mistake, use your command. Repeat this phase over several days.

Phase Four

The shake of the cup should now be very subtle. When your pup looks at the correct person, give your command using the correct name before you release him. Continue to treat him liberally if he goes to the correct place.

If your pup makes a mistake and goes to the incorrect person, that person should just stand still and look away. Never chastise the pup, as this will damage his confidence in playing the game.

Continue to do a series with one person. Then switch to the other person and do several repetitions.

Phase Five

Gradually fade the food shaking. Use your command and send your pup. Throw a party if he goes directly to the correct person.

Gradually fade the food shaking in the "Where's John?" game and simply use your command to send your pup to the proper person.

Phase Six

When your pup consistently runs to the correct person on command, you have two directions you can go. One option is to add an additional person. Start back at the first step to teach your pup the new name. It will go faster this time because your pup understands the game.

The other option is to increase the distance to the people so that your pup actually searches for the correct person. If he stumbles onto the incorrect person, that person should just stay quiet and look away rather than trying to tell the pup what to do. Then wait for your pup to track down the correct person.

Trainer Talk

Although your pup's attention span is longer now, it is still important to know when to end the game. Where's John? is so cute that it is easy to play excessively. Remember to stop playing, or switch games, before your pup quits. He should end every activity begging to do more.

Possible Challenges

If your pup gets anxious at any time and races back and forth between your friends, trying to get treats from both, go back to the previous practice level. He is showing that he doesn't yet understand that going to just one person is "correct." He is trying to offer a comfortable behavior to see if it will earn a treat.

Exercise #36: High Five

Goal: Teach your pup to raise his paw to give you a high-five slap on your palm.
Ideal Age to Start: 10 months
Groundwork: Your dog should have a solid *sit*.
Clicker: No

Background

Teaching a pup to shake hands with a friend has been a traditional dog trick. It is easy to teach by simply grasping your dog's collar and rocking him gently to the side while he is sitting. When he lifts his paw, grasp it while you use your marker word. Then release his paw and deliver his cookie. This violates our rule of treating the dog while he is doing the behavior we want, but it is practically impossible to do initially because both your hands

Real-Life Pups

It took no time at all to teach this pup to high five. Since she had already learned to shake, she was quick to raise her paw when confronted with the cookie in her handler's hand. From that point, she figured out the new game in no time.

are busy. The good news is that most dogs enjoy shaking hands so much that this variation doesn't seem to matter.

Pups should never volunteer to shake on their own because pawing when someone approaches can become a nuisance behavior. If your pup does start flailing his paw as someone comes toward him, turn around and walk him away. Only let the pup shake when he is able to control himself until you give the command.

The *high five* is a hipper version of *shake*. The pup lifts his paw high enough to slap his pad on your palm. Unlike the shake, which is used to greet a friend, the *high-five* game is generally played only between handler and pup. It is a lovely game to celebrate some success with your canine pal. It says: *What a team!*

Process

Phase One

1. Put a high-powered treat in your hand and close it.
2. Give your pup the *sit* command. With your pup seated in front of you, hold your fist at about nose level. He will likely nose your hand first. Just ignore that.
3. If your dog gets up, quietly ask him to sit again. Praise but don't treat when he does. Just hold steady until he paws at your hand.
4. Immediately open your hand and release the treat to him. You can click the pawing, or just mark it verbally.

If your dog is just baffled about what you want, try lowering your hand. Then use a soft tap behind his lower leg. My younger dog Boo kept trying everything he knew to get the treat until I indicated that it had something to do with his leg. Then the lightbulb went on and he slapped a paw at my fist, which was just a few inches (cm) from the ground.

Phase Two

1. Open your hand a bit, but hide the treat under your bent fingers. Face your palm toward your pup with your fingers up. Repeat the game as described in Phase One.
2. When he paws your hand, deliver the treat.

The *high five* teaches your pup to lift his paw high enough to slap his pad on your palm.

Trainer Talk

Long ago we talked about the importance of problem solving in any puppy training. When you hit a challenge with your pup, stop whatever you are doing. Never let yourself get frustrated, because that will make your pup anxious. Switch gears from trainer to problem solver. With my pup Scout, I asked myself: *What can I use to get her excited enough to paw but not so excited that she loses her mind?* When you are teaching *high five* or other commands, consider what clever thing you can do that would get your pup to do what you want. Once you get the behavior you want, tell the pup how much you like it by using your clicker or marker word and reward, reward, reward.

3. Start to use your command *high five* right after he paws.

Phase Three
1. Open your hand and face your palm toward your pup.
2. If he slaps it, mark and treat. If he hesitates, repeat with a treat slipped between your fingers. Make sure that he doesn't get it by nosing you.
3. Use your *high-five* command while he is pawing.

Phase Four
Now you can cue with your open hand only. Use your command before he starts to paw.

Phase Five
For dogs whose backs aren't too long (which puts them at higher risk for a back injury), it is possible to teach a *high-ten* command with both paws hitting both your hands. My dogs think *high five* is plenty, but dogs who enjoy sitting up on their haunches are naturals for *high ten*. This is a sitting game, though. Don't encourage your dog to leap while doing this—you don't want him to think that he is getting permission to jump on you.

Possible Challenges
There are two types of dogs that are challenged by this game. Some dogs who are very scent oriented have trouble with this game. They just want to keep poking at that treat with their nose. Hold the treat lower and see if you can get the pup to lift his paw at all. If he does, immediately mark and release the treat. Then very slowly move the treat higher.

This game can be a challenge with dogs who get crazy in the presence of food. For example, my older Sheltie Scout got so excited about the food locked in my hand that she kept assuming I wanted her to lie down. She was so wound up she wouldn't try doing something else. After thinking about this for a while, I quit using food and held a teensy tennis ball that she loves to play with in my hand. This made her think, and finally she reached out with a paw. From that point on, I used the toy to teach her the command.

Exercise #37: Back

Goal: Teach your dog to back up in a straight line.
Ideal Age to Start: 10 months
Groundwork: No
Clicker: Yes

Background

Dogs are body language experts. They understand movement much more than spoken language. Teaching your dog a variety of tricks such as *back* is a great way to get attuned to each other's movement.

In this trick, one of you moves back and the other moves forward. Then you switch roles. This is a great first game in learning to dance together. If you ever decide to participate in the dog sport called canine freestyle, this is a move you could incorporate into your routine with your dog.

Process

Phase One

1. To get started, teach your dog to back up by walking him through a "chute." A chute can be made by placing, for example, two picnic benches on their sides parallel to each other, leaving just enough width for him to walk through.
2. Put some treats in your hand. Begin by backing through the chute yourself and luring your dog to follow you through. Walk him forward three to five times and reward him while he is inside the chute. Make sure that he is comfortable walking forward in the chute before you start working on the *back* command.
3. Next, face your pup and walk toward him while both of you are in the chute. Hold your hands in front of your thighs or your pup will think that you want him to sit. Begin by clicking and rewarding him for the tiniest movement backward—even a half step. To reinforce, just turn your hand over and give him the treat inside. If he gets confused and sits down, try bending over slightly to lower your hands. Next, click and reward for one full step backward, and then gradually progress to two steps back.

Phase Two
Once your dog is comfortable backing

Trainer Talk

Trainers often use different tools called "barriers" to control a dog's position. In this game, the picnic benches are barriers that help the pup understand that you want him to back up. It is often useful to use a barrier such as a wall to help a pup learn to sit or lie down straight at your side.

up through the chute, practice walking toward him so that he has to back up, and then back up so that he walks toward you. You and your dog will look like you are dancing the cha cha. Start using your *back* command when your pup is in the process of backing up.

Phase Three
When your dog is good at this game, it is time to transition to backing without the barriers. Simply widen the barriers over time until they are so far apart that they are no longer containing your dog and he is backing up on his own.

As you wean him from the barriers, continue to alternate moving backward and forward so that he has to move both toward you and away from you. During this phase, use your command to initiate the *back* behavior.

Possible Challenges
The biggest challenge in this exercise is finding barriers to contain your dog while he learns to back. Picnic benches are the best, but a sofa scooted close to a wall forms a nice backing chute too. Once you figure out which barriers work, this is an easy, fun game.

Exercise #38: Jump and Off
Goal: Teach your pup to jump up on and off an object.
Ideal Age to Start: 11 months for low jumps; 12 to 15 months for higher jumps. Long-backed dogs such as Dachshunds should not play this game, because they are prone to back problems.
Groundwork: No
Clicker: Yes

Background
In general, dogs love to spring up on things. Jumping must be approached cautiously with young dogs so that they don't damage their growth plates. This is a game that should begin when your pup is well into his adolescence, with jumps at low heights. Once your pup is mature physically, you will find that he loves this game of springing onto surfaces that you indicate.

Once your pup is on the object, you must next clearly teach the reverse. When you taught the *lap* command (Exercise #6), you taught your pup the *off* command, too. He will pick it up again quickly in this game.

Occasionally, folks worry about teaching this command to their pup if he is prone to jumping on them. This is not a concern. If your

Real-Life Pups
In this photo you see a young Jack Russell Terrier learning to back up. The handler is doing an excellent job of keeping her hands low, to keep the pup from sitting. The handler is moving into her pup slowly to put her in reverse gear.

communication with him is clear, your pup can easily discriminate between jumping on a bench and not jumping on you.

Process

Phase One
Start by locating a flat object that is no higher than your pup's elbows and that's big enough for him to land on comfortably. If you have a big puppy, recruit a friend to help.

1. Walk your pup on leash up to the object.
2. Have your friend hold your treats at the far edge of the object and pat the surface invitingly. Most pups will put their front feet up to check out the treats.
3. As soon as he does, give him a bite and gently hoist his rear end onto the object.
4. As soon as all feet are up, click and give several treats. This tells

If you clearly communicate with your pup, he will easily be able to discriminate between jumping on an object and not jumping on you.

him clearly that you like it when he gets up on the object. If your pup just happens to spring all the way onto the object, click and treat.
5. After reinforcing your pup while he is on the object, give your *off* command and lure your pup to jump off.

Phase Two
Once your pup shows that he is comfortable putting his front feet up, you are ready to up the ante.

1. Walk your pup on leash up to the object and toss the treat onto the back of the object rather than giving it to your friend. Most pups will still respond by putting up their front feet and trying to reach for it.
2. If yours does this, hoist, click, and treat. The next time you bring him back and do the same thing, he will likely jump onto the object to get the treat. If he doesn't, continue to lift him up until he understands what you want.

During this phase, start saying your command word "jump" after your pup is on the table. Use your *off* command just after he is safely on the floor.

Trainer Talk

Like humans, dogs have a plate at the end of each bone that allows the bone to grow. The growth plates are quite delicate until they close. For toy breeds, this happens at about 12 months, and for large breeds, this happens at about 15 months. If you are curious, your vet can check the status of your pup's growth plates. Be cautious about any activity that puts a lot of pressure on the bones because the growth plates can be damaged. For example, don't let your pup jump out of a tall truck or SUV.

Phase Three

Once your pup is consistently leaping onto the surface, it's time to wean him from luring.
1. Continue to pat the table invitingly. When your pup jumps up, click and treat. It is a good strategy to toss the treats onto the "table" as he is jumping so that he continues to think of it as a magic place.
2. It is time to use both commands while your dog is in transit. In this case, say "Jump" while your dog is in the air on the way up and "Off" when he is on the way down.

Phase Four

When your pup is clearly eager to jump on a designated object, it's time to use your commands before he jumps on and off.

You can help your pup generalize the command by finding a variety of things of appropriate heights on which to practice. For example, a nearby park has large flat rocks that my pups always find entertaining for jumping.

Once your pup reaches physical maturity, you can gradually increase the height of the jumps. Healthy dogs can easily jump onto objects as tall as they are.

Phase Five

A strong pup can jump very effectively from a *sit*. Once your pup has lots of experience jumping, walk him up to an object with which he is familiar, have him sit, and then ask him to jump. Many pups can spring almost cat-like from a *sit* onto a "table."

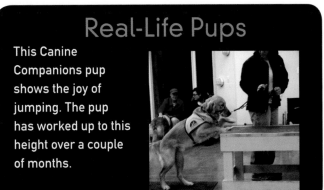

Real-Life Pups

This Canine Companions pup shows the joy of jumping. The pup has worked up to this height over a couple of months.

Possible Challenges

If you have worked on having your pup stay off the furniture, he may be reluctant to put his feet up on the objects. If he is, gently lift his front legs up onto the object and treat him. Then gently hoist the rest of his body up, click, and reinforce. Most dogs quickly learn that this is an approved game and not something for which they will get in trouble.

Occasionally, pups just refuse to jump even when the jump is quite low. This has often proven to be a physical issue and not a question of stubbornness. If your dog clearly says no to this game, a physical examination might be in order before you proceed.

Exercise #39: Spin Right and Left

Goal: Teach your pup to spin quickly in a 360-degree circle.
Ideal Age to Start: 12 months
Groundwork: Casual *Heel* (Exercise #14)
Clicker: Yes

Background

This is a game many pups particularly enjoy. If you have any interest in the dog sport of canine freestyle, a type of choreographed obedience/dance routine with your dog, the *spin* is a move you will find easy to incorporate. There's nothing cuter than a pup who knows how to pirouette on command while you are walking together.

Process

Phase One

1. Put your pup next to you on either side—no need for a *sit*.
2. Put a treat in the hand closest to the pup. Get his attention with the cookie at his nose.
3. Lure him to turn his head away from you. Continue to draw a circle with a treat until he completes a 360-degree *spin*. Move the lure slowly enough that he can follow it.

Trainer Talk

One of the most endearing behaviors that you will observe with your puppy during training is something called "offering behaviors." Imagine that you take a treat out of your pocket to help your pup learn the command *spin*. Before you can even do anything, you may find that your pup gets so excited that he quickly sits, downs, and high fives (assuming you have taught those behaviors) as he tries to figure out what you want him to do and how he can earn that cookie. As puppies mature they figure out that they have to listen to the command first, and offering behaviors fade away.

4. Use your clicker to mark the completion of the *spin* and deliver your treat.
5. Repeat for several sessions.
6. Next, put your pup on your other side. Remember to put the treat in the hand closest to the pup. Lure his head away from you and complete the *spin*.

Many puppies turn easily in one direction but have a harder time spinning in the other direction. Like people, pups tend to have a dominant side. This makes it important to practice both directions so that the pup is balanced physically. You may need to move your treat more slowly on the pup's "stiffer" side until he gets comfortable with turning in that direction.

The *spin* is a good foundation for canine freestyle, or doggy dancing.

Phase Two
1. Repeat the game as in Phase One, but add your verbal cue, "spin," just as he completes the *spin*. (You can use the same *spin* command on both sides.)
2. Click and treat.
3. Once your dog is spinning easily, it is time to use your command while he is making the turn.
4. Start to fade the lure, and begin to use your hand to cue your pup that he is going to spin. Use your hand to draw the correct path for the pup. Alternate this with an occasional lure.
5. Make sure to click and reward a completed *spin*. Be especially generous if your pup made the circle without being lured.

Phase Three
1. Repeat the game again using your verbal cue before your pup starts the behavior. Help him with a lure initially so that he gets it right and then gradually fade the lure. When you are not luring, continue to use your hand to draw the path.
2. As always, remember to click and treat.

Real-Life Pups

This photo shows a young Labrador learning to spin. This handler is using a cookie to lure her since the pup is just beginning this game.

Some herding breeds spin as a default behavior when they get very excited.

Phase Four

If you want, you can add movement now.

1. Walk with your puppy next to your left side in a casual *heel*. Because this will be a new picture for your pup, go back to using a treat in the hand closest to him.
2. Get his attention with the cookie at his nose and lure him to turn his head away from you. Continue to draw a circle with a treat until he completes a 360-degree *spin*.
3. Use your clicker to mark the completion of the spin and deliver your treat. Keep moving forward.
4. It will not take him long to get comfortable with the spin while moving if you have taken enough time on the stationary spin. Once he appears confident, eliminate your food lure and just cue the *spin* with your hand.

Phase Five

Once your pup understands the game, you can fade the cue with your hand.

1. Since you have been drawing the full *spin* circle with your hand, start to shorten the path

that you draw. For a few sessions, draw 80 percent of the path, then 60 percent, then 40 percent. You will get to a point that the verbal command and the tiniest flick of your finger will get your pup to spin.

2. Fade the finger movement altogether.
3. Now you can play with this behavior in a couple of ways. Ask for a *spin* whenever you want to add a little excitement to your walk. When you are waiting around for your turn in puppy class, have your pup spin right and left to keep him focused on you.

Possible Challenges

Some herding breeds spin as a default behavior when they get very excited. This is something a pup does when he is overly stimulated or when he doesn't understand what you are asking. If you have an obsessive spinner, you might want to skip this game. However, there are exceptions. Some dogs who are prone to spinning always turn in one direction. In this case, teaching the *spin* in the opposite direction would be useful to keep the pup balanced physically.

Exercise #40: Do What Comes Naturally

Goal: Select a game that your pup plays naturally and teach him to do it on command.
Ideal Age to Start: 12 months
Groundwork: Observe your pup for behaviors that he repeats and seems to enjoy. Select one that would make a good "trick."
Clicker: Yes, if you have it handy when your dog offers the behavior. Otherwise, use your marker word and reinforce with treats.

Background

Different dogs have types of behaviors that come easily. For example, some dogs make a lovely little yodeling sound. This is easy to teach with a *talk pretty* command. Some dogs love to initiate a game by laying their front legs down and keeping their behind elevated. If this is your dog, mark the behavior with a *take a bow* command. The possibilities are endless.

Start to watch your pup for what comes naturally. If he likes to carry things, teach him to carry a paper bag with your lunch (rather than eating it). If he likes to use his paws, teach him to salute. If he likes to press his head on your leg, teach him the command *visit*. You get the point. This is a great opportunity to practice independently what you have learned about dog training.

Process

Phase One

Keep your clicker and some treats in your pocket. Once you have identified when you are likely to see the behavior, get ready.

1. As soon as your pup does it, click and treat. For example, if your pup does a *play bow*, click while he is bowing and then reinforce with a cookie. If you can, give the treat while your dog is still bowing, but if you can't, just reward as soon as possible after the click.
2. Repeat 30 to 50 times.

It's relatively easy to teach your dog a behavior that comes naturally, such as the *play bow*.

Remember not to use any words during this first phase. Just use that click or marker word to tell your pup how much you like that behavior.

Phase Two
Select a word you want to use for the command and start using it just after the behavior. If your dog is having fun with this game, you should start to see him offering the behavior on his own more often.

Phase Three
Start using your command during the behavior. Continue to click and reinforce with a cookie.

Real-Life Pups
With my youngest Sheltie pup, I captured an interesting behavior. One day I was two-stepping around the house to a Western song. I was moving backward and he started walking toward me. Tentatively he jumped on me. I put my hands down with my palms across from his paws. He found them and kept walking toward me on his hind legs. Bingo, I thought. With a bit of practice, we dance regularly now, and he gets very excited when I ask him, "Want to dance?" He is the perfect partner because he never steps on my toes. I do my best to steer clear of his.

Phase Four

As you well know, you may start using the command to initiate the behavior once your pup has shown you that he understands the game. Move to this phase only when you feel 100 percent certain that he will respond appropriately.

Possible Challenges

If you choose to teach your pup a complex trick, one that requires more than one behavior, it is important that he understands each of the parts first. Do you remember when we discussed the need to focus on one variable at time? It is easy to confuse a pup if you lump too many things together. It's like asking a child to write a word before understanding letters.

When you think of something you would like to teach your pup, split it into distinct parts. For example, imagine that you would like to teach your dog to turn off light switches on the wall. He would first need to learn to paw at an object persistently. Then he would need to learn to balance against the wall on his hind legs. Then you could connect the two behaviors.

Trainer Talk

Pups can learn very complex behaviors. The challenge to you as a trainer is to learn to break these behaviors down into individual components. This takes some practice. Imagine that you want to teach your pup to open a door by pulling on a rope. How many individual things would you need to teach? The answer is three: First the pup must grasp the rope; then he needs to tug on it; and third, he must understand how to back up. Each of these should be taught separately and then combined.

Afterword
A Good Dog Mind Is a Terrible Thing to Waste

Teaching a pup intensively throughout his first year creates a partner who is smarter and more responsive than you ever imagined.

Many chapters ago, I set out to convince you that all puppyhoods are not created equal. I hope *The Gifted Puppy Program* has implanted (or reinforced) three fundamental beliefs about puppy raising:

1. Teaching a pup intensively throughout his first year creates a partner who is smarter and more responsive than you ever imagined.
2. Pups are happiest when they are actively learning new things and practicing familiar games with you.
3. Teaching your pup has deepened your relationship in a way that just hanging out together never would have done.

If you have followed the program, I trust that you are proud that your pup has had an extraordinary upbringing. I have found that once folks try this approach to raising a pup, they can't imagine having done it any other way.

You may wonder how the pups shown throughout the book to demonstrate different games and commands have grown up. Jade, the Border Collie pup, is all grown up at the completion of this manuscript. Jade is still an exuberant girl who grins at everyone she meets and approaches everything she does with joie de vivre. All of Lauri's socialization with Jade paid off. The girl is very comfortable wherever she goes. Jade still notices loud sounds that used to scare her, but she has learned enough self-control to stay focused on Lauri. Although Lauri knew when she added Jade to her family that she was headed for a career in agility, she continues to teach and practice the basics and beyond. Lauri says, "Giving her a solid obedience foundation was the smartest thing I did."

The Canine Companions pups featured in the book were all returned to CCI when they turned 16 months old. Advanced training to become an assistance dog is quite strenuous and requires perfection in every way. Some graduated and went on to serve people with a variety of disabilities. Others were returned to their puppy raisers and have changed careers to become therapy dogs, agility dogs, and beloved pets.

I believe that every day our dogs spend with us is a gift. What I try to give back to them is a guarantee that their lives will be fun, stimulating, and challenging in appropriate ways. It means that part of every day is dedicated to enjoying our partnership and exploring new things that we can learn or play together. My dogs are poking me in the leg right now reminding me that it is time to make good on my promise. It is an invitation I can't resist. I hope you will head out to play and work with your gifted dog, too.

Appendix I
Socialization Plan

Remember to discuss your plan for socialization with your veterinarian. Pups are not fully protected until they receive their final puppy shot at about four months. Because the time up to 16 weeks is a critical window for socialization, you must find a balance between protecting your pup and providing him with adequate experiences so that he feels comfortable in the world.

There are situations you should avoid with your pup and possibly continue to avoid throughout his entire life. These include noisy events such as firework displays, parades, and concerts. Most dogs simply find these overwhelming.

Age of Pup (Weeks)	Appropriate Socialization Opportunities	Notes
Week 8	Walks around your yard and a quiet street. Have friends come to visit. Take rides in the car in crate. Carry your pup while you go to the ATM.	Never walk where you might encounter loose dogs who might scare your pup.
Weeks 9 and 10	Expand your walks a bit farther in your neighborhood, start a puppy kindergarten class, take rides in the car, and walk to quiet locations such as the bank. Carry your pup into a small pet store. Visit with kind people you meet.	Make sure that pups are sorted by size to play in your kindergarten class. Large pups should never be allowed to bully smaller pups.
Weeks 11 and 12	Walk your pup around small, quiet strip malls or visit a pet or feed store and walk your pup around. Let him look at chickens and kitties. Interact with as many different people as possible. Take your pup to visit friends.	As you go out to public places and friends' houses, remember to monitor your pup's housetraining so that he doesn't make a mistake.
Weeks 13 to 16	Walk your pup regularly around busier shopping centers such as those with a supermarket. Continue to find opportunities for your pup to interact with calm pups and dogs. Take longer trips in the car. If you plan to participate in a dog sport such as agility or rally, take your pup to one or more events.	Introductions should be handled so that your pup is never fearful. Make sure on your outings that your pup is walking nicely on leash and greeting people appropriately.
Week 17 to 1 year	Start to walk your pup on busier streets. By six or seven months, most pups are ready to walk on downtown streets. Shop regularly in dog-friendly stores. Dine with your pup under the table at outdoor restaurants. Continue to attend puppy training classes.	If your pup becomes anxious in any setting, take your next outing to somewhere a bit less stimulating. Return to the original location in a week or so. Take lots of treats to reward him if he relaxes.

Appendix II
Your Sporty Pup

Serious training for dog sports does not generally begin until after a pup is at least a year old and his growth plates are closed. However, most trainers teach foundation skills to young pups in order to lay the groundwork for more advanced training. Remember that it is okay to start these games when your pup is older, though, if you want to try new things.

Since you are now an experienced trainer, I have shortened the instructions for each activity.

#1: Balancing Act (Agility Prep)
Goal: Teach your pup to stand with all four feet on a balance disc.

Background
This exercise teaches super balance and coordination. It is excellent preparation for future agility pups, who will need to ride a teeter-totter to the ground. It is also fun for all pups. It does require a special prop, which is known as a balance disc. The discs are air-filled cushions that look like a circular chair pad. During this game, you are going to teach your pup to stand on the disc, first with two feet and then, if you are ambitious, with all four feet.

Process
1. You will teach this game by shaping. First, teach your pup to approach the disc. Try to click while the pup is moving toward the disc or even glancing at it. Toss the treat near the disc.
2. Most pups will be curious once they are near the disc and will try to interact with it. Click and treat anything such as looking at it, nose touching, or foot lifting.
3. Next, try tossing the treat to the opposite side of the disc so that the pup has to walk around it. There is a huge chance the pup will brush the disc with a foot. If so, click during this moment and throw a second treat to the opposite side of the disc. Never pick up the pup and place him on the disc. Let him learn on his own that it is rewarding to stand on the disc because you will click and treat

that action. This may take several days, so be patient.

4. Once your pup has figured out that he can get two paws on the disc, you can teach him to stand on the disc with all four paws. Watch for him to make any effort to put his hind foot on the disc. If he touches it, click and reinforce liberally. Gradually raise the bar so that you click and treat each movement toward getting another foot on. When he does, throw a party. Try to work up to having your pup balance for at least 15 to 30 seconds.

#2: Walk the Plank (Agility Prep)

Goal: Your dog walks or trots across a board 12 inches (.3 m) wide with all four feet on the board from end to end.

Background

If you are thinking about doing agility someday, your dog will learn to run across an obstacle called the dogwalk in your agility class. This is a long "catwalk" that is just 12 inches (.3 m) wide. To do this successfully, dogs must learn to stay on something that is quite narrow while they are moving quickly. To play this game, put a board 12 inches (.3 m) wide on two cement blocks. The board can be any length. The blocks will elevate the board about 1 foot (.3 m) off the ground.

Process

1. With your puppy on leash, approach the plank and see if he is interested in putting his feet on it or interested in walking or trotting on it. Many dogs will happily jump up and walk along the plank of their own accord. If your dog is one of these pups, allow him to walk or trot along the length of the board as you walk next to him. Praise him as he travels, and treat him at the end of the board before you let him jump off.

2. If you have played Meet the Goblins (Physical Objects)(Exercise #21), which encourages your pup to interact with objects, he will likely approach the board with confidence. But if your dog is hesitant, bring out your clicker. Begin by clicking for any interest he shows in putting his feet on the board. It is best if he chooses to get on himself. However, if you are patient and he doesn't get on by himself, you can lure him on with food and then place treats along the board to get him comfortable with moving on it.

3. Gradually progress to walking alongside the board, and fade the use of the clicker for the time being. Progress until you can run alongside as your dog trots or gallops across the plank.

#3: Capture the Disc (Disc Dog Prep)

Goal: Teach a pup that chasing a disc and bringing it back is rewarding.

Background

If you hope to have your pup grow into a dog who will chase and return flying discs, you must work on two key skills while he is young. First, having a pup who comes back to you when called is essential. Play all the *recall* games in the book regularly for many months so that your youngster will turn on a dime when called. The second thing of importance is to introduce your pup to the disc in a way that captures his interest.

It is tempting to just start throwing the disc, but this is not a good idea. Because of their poor vision, pups often lose track of a thrown flying disc and learn to ignore the toy rather than getting excited. This game allows the pup to track the toy and chase it consistently.

Make sure to select a disc, like one Nylabone makes, that is an appropriate size and type for your pup. There are hard plastic discs, squishy discs, and even soft glow-in-the-dark discs. My Shelties, for example, prefer a softer disc that is about 8 inches (20.5 cm) in diameter.

Lastly, never leave the disc out as a toy for your pup. It should always be a special toy that you two play with together. If your pup has continuous access, the toy is likely to become ho-hum.

Process

1. Start with your pup on the long line so that he doesn't get jerked back by the leash if the disc goes farther away than you expect. Get your pup's attention with a happy voice or by slapping the disc on the ground in an enticing way.
2. As he looks at you, roll the disc on its edge a short distance. Let your pup chase it. Stay quiet as he follows it, jumps on it, or grabs it. If your pup brings it back, terrific—tell him how brilliant he is and trade the disc for a treat.
3. If he doesn't bring the toy back, let him play with it for several seconds and then very slowly and gently reel him in. Tell him what a good pup he is. Exchange the disc for a treat if he holds on. If he lets go, praise him, deliver a treat, and toss the toy again.

#4: Leg Weaves (Freestyle Prep)

Goal: Teach your dog to weave in and out of your legs while you walk slowly. Your goal is to take at least four steps while your pup weaves.

Background

Freestyle is doing tricks to music and putting it all together to tell a story. The joy of freestyle is that mixed breeds, purebreds, dogs of any size, and dogs of any age can participate. Even dogs who have had to retire from another sport because of an injury have an entire new world of training to explore.

You can start this game at sixth months for small and medium dogs, but if your dog has a long back, wait until a year to avoid twisting his back. Giant breeds might not be able to play this game.

Process

1. Get a treat in both hands.
2. Next, take one big step forward. Using a treat, lure your dog through from the inside to the outside of your leg.
3. Take another big step and lure the dog through that leg from inside to outside. Repeat over several days.
4. Next, get two treats in each hand. Start as you did before and simply add a third and fourth step. Gradually drop the lure and cue the weave with your hand.

#5: Harness Up (Skijoring/Sledding Prep)

Goal: Teach your pup to wear a harness and run ahead of you.

Background

The tradition of teaching dogs to pull is alive and well. Sled dog racing and skijoring, a cross between sled dog racing and cross country skiing, have a devoted following in areas with snow. In recent years, skijoring has expanded to bikejoring, skatejoring, and even scooterjoring. Okay, I made up that last word, but there really are scooters available that are adapted to allow you to hook your dog up for some pulling power.

Obviously, not all dogs are candidates for sled dog work, but you might be surprised how many dogs enjoy playing. There are terrific teams of Dalmatians, Coonhounds, and Border Collies. I drove a Golden Retriever/Labrador cross, a Wolfhound cross, and a German Shorthaired Pointer, along with a variety of northern breeds. If you have a medium to large dog who likes to run, this may be your game.

It is important to remember that dogs should not be allowed to pull weight until their growth plates are closed. This game is fine, however, because your pup won't actually haul anything. Second, make sure to purchase a harness that fits your dog. Many websites sell them, and help is readily available to measure your dog for a good fit. Beware of asking him to pull on asphalt, because it's hard on the paws, or in areas with traffic.

You may wonder about teaching your pup to pull when you have worked so hard to teach him to walk next to you. Pups can learn to discriminate between the two behaviors: When I have my collar on, I walk nicely, but when I have my harness on, I get to run ahead and pull. However, it is best to teach a good *heel* first rather than teaching the pup to pull first.

Process

1. Slip the harness gently on your pup. Take him for a walk with it on. Make sure that it fits so that nothing rubs. Let him wear the harness during walks for several days.
2. Once he is comfortable wearing the harness, find a lively friend. It is going to be her job to run ahead of you and your pup with a desired toy or treat.

3. Harness your pup. Hook your leash to the loop closest to your pup's tail. When you start moving, make sure not to wrap the leash around your hands or your waist, because you could get hurt.
4. Have your friend show your pup the toy or treat and run ahead a short distance. She can use your pup's name. Your pup will move away from you and toward your friend. Trail behind with the leash taut but without applying much pressure. Odds are good that you will have to run.
5. Have your friend give the pup a cookie when he gets there. Then hold your pup while your friend runs away again. Increase the distance in short increments. Repeat the game. As your pup gets confident, your friend can go farther and farther ahead. She can also start running while the pup is moving, as long as you and your pup can eventually catch her.
6. When your pup is confident with this game, he will be ready to start pulling once he is physically ready.

If your dog is reluctant to run away from you in a harness, there are two things to try: First, switch positions with your partner. It is highly likely that your pup will want to run to you. Once your pup understands the joy of racing forward in the harness, switch back. Second, find a clearly defined trail. Dogs love following a path, so this may turn your pup on more than an open field does.

Resources

Associations and Organizations

Breed Clubs

American Kennel Club (AKC)
8051 Arco Corporate Drive, Suite 100
Raleigh, NC 27617-3390
Telephone: (919) 233-9767
Fax: (919) 233-3627
E-Mail: info@akc.org
www.akc.org

Canadian Kennel Club (CKC)
200 Ronson Drive, Suite 400
Etobicoke, Ontario M9W 5Z9
Telephone: (416) 675-5511
Fax: (416) 675-6506
E-Mail: information@ckc.ca
www.ckc.ca

Fédération Cynologique Internationale (FCI)
FCI Office
Place Albert 1er, 13
B – 6530 Thuin
Belgique
Telephone: +32 71 59.12.38
Fax: +32 71 59.22.29
www.fci.be

The Kennel Club
1-5 Clarges Street, Piccadilly, London W1J 8AB
Telephone: 0844 463 3980
Fax: 020 7518 1028
www.thekennelclub.org.uk

United Kennel Club (UKC)
100 E. Kilgore Road
Kalamazoo, MI 49002-5584
Telephone: (269) 343-9020
Fax: (269) 343-7037
www.ukcdogs.com

Pet Sitters

National Association of Professional Pet Sitters (NAPPS)
15000 Commerce Parkway, Suite C
Mt. Laurel, New Jersey 08054
Telephone: (856) 439-0324
Fax: (856) 439-0525
E-Mail: napps@petsitters.org
www.petsitters.org

Pet Sitters International
201 East King Street
King, NC 27021-9161
Telephone: (336) 983-9222
Fax: (336) 983-5266
E-Mail: info@petsit.com
www.petsit.com

Rescue Organizations and Animal Welfare Groups

American Humane Association
1400 16th Street NW, Suite 360
Washington, DC 20036
Telephone: (800) 227-4645
E-Mail: info@americanhumane.org
www.americanhumane.org

American Society for the Prevention of Cruelty to Animals (ASPCA)
424 E. 92nd Street
New York, NY 10128-6804
Telephone: (212) 876-7700
www.aspca.org

Royal Society for the Prevention of Cruelty to Animals (RSPCA)
RSPCA Advice Team
Wilberforce Way
Southwater
Horsham
West Sussex
RH13 9RS
United Kingdom
Telephone: 0300 1234 999
www.rspca.org.uk

Sports

International Agility Link (IAL)
85 Blackwall Road
Chuwar, Queensland
Australia 4306
Telephone: 61 (07) 3202 2361
Fax: 61 (07) 3281 6872
Email: steve@agilityclick.com
www.agilityclick.com/~ial/

The North American Dog Agility Council (NADAC)
24605 Dodds Rd.
Bend, Oregon 97701
www.nadac.com

North American Flyball Association (NAFA)
1333 West Devon Avenue, #512
Chicago, IL 60660
Telephone: (800) 318-6312
Fax: (800) 318-6312
Email: flyball@flyball.org
www.flyball.org

United States Dog Agility Association (USDAA)
P.O. Box 850955
Richardson, TX 75085
Telephone: (972) 487-2200
Fax: (972) 231-9700
www.usdaa.com

The World Canine Freestyle Organization, Inc.
P.O. Box 350122
Brooklyn, NY 11235
Telephone: (718) 332-8336
Fax: (718) 646-2686
E-Mail: WCFODOGS@aol.com
www.worldcaninefreestyle.org

Therapy

Pet Partners
875 124th Ave, NE, Suite 101
Bellevue, WA 98005
Telephone: (425) 679-5500
Fax: (425) 679-5539
E-Mail: info@petpartners.org
www.petpartners.org

Therapy Dogs Inc.
P.O. Box 20227
Cheyenne, WY 82003
Telephone: (877) 843-7364
Fax: (307) 638-2079
E-Mail: therapydogsinc@qwestoffice.net
www.therapydogs.com

Therapy Dogs International (TDI)
88 Bartley Road
Flanders, NJ 07836
Telephone: (973) 252-9800
Fax: (973) 252-7171
E-Mail: tdi@gti.net
www.tdi-dog.org

Training

American College of Veterinary Behaviorists (ACVB)
College of Veterinary Medicine, 4474 TAMU
Texas A&M University
College Station, Texas 77843-4474
www.dacvb.org

American Kennel Club Canine Health Foundation, Inc. (CHF)
P. O. Box 900061
Raleigh, NC 27675
Telephone: (888) 682-9696
Fax: (919) 334-4011
www.akcchf.org

Association of Professional Dog Trainers (APDT)
104 South Calhoun Street
Greenville, SC 29601
Telephone: (800) PET-DOGS
Fax: (864) 331-0767
E-Mail: information@apdt.com
www.apdt.com

International Association of Animal Behavior Consultants (IAABC)
565 Callery Road
Cranberry Township, PA 16066
E-Mail: info@iaabc.org
www.iaabc.org

National Association of Dog Obedience Instructors (NADOI)
7910 Picador Drive
Houston, TX 77083-4918
Telephone: (972) 296-1196
E-Mail: info@nadoi.org
www.nadoi.org

Veterinary and Health Resources

The Academy of Veterinary Homeopathy (AVH)
P. O. Box 232282
Leucadia, CA 92023-2282
Telephone: (866) 652-1590
Fax: (866) 652-1590
www.theavh.org

American Academy of Veterinary Acupuncture (AAVA)
P.O. Box 1058
Glastonbury, CT 06033
Telephone: (860) 632-9911
www.aava.org

American Animal Hospital Association (AAHA)
12575 W. Bayaud Ave.
Lakewood, CO 80228
Telephone: (303) 986-2800
Fax: (303) 986-1700
E-Mail: info@aahanet.org
www.aahanet.org

American College of Veterinary Internal Medicine (ACVIM)
1997 Wadsworth Blvd., Suite A
Lakewood, CO 80214-5293
Telephone: 303-231-9933
Telephone (US or Canada): (800) 245-9081
Fax: (303) 231-0880
Email: ACVIM@ACVIM.org
www.acvim.org

American College of Veterinary Ophthalmologists (ACVO)
P.O. Box 1311
Meridian, ID 83860
Telephone: (208) 466-7624
Fax: (208) 466-7693
E-Mail: office13@acvo.com
www.acvo.org

American Heartworm Society (AHS)
P.O. Box 8266
Wilmington, DE 19803-8266
Email: info@heartwormsociety.org
www.heartwormsociety.org

American Holistic Veterinary Medical Association (AHVMA)
P. O. Box 630
Abingdon, MD 21009-0630
Telephone: (410) 569-0795
Fax: (410) 569-2346
E-Mail: office@ahvma.org
www.ahvma.org

American Veterinary Medical Association (AVMA)
1931 North Meacham Road, Suite 100
Schaumburg, IL 60173-4360
Telephone: (800) 248-2862
Fax: (847) 925-1329
www.avma.org

ASPCA Animal Poison Control Center
Telephone: (888) 426-4435
www.aspca.org

British Veterinary Association (BVA)
7 Mansfield Street
London
W1G 9NQ
Telephone: 020 7636 6541
Fax: 020 7908 6349
E-Mail: bvahq@bva.co.uk
www.bva.co.uk

Canine Eye Registration Foundation (CERF)
P.O. Box 199
Rantoul, Il 61866-0199
Telephone: (217) 693-4800
Fax: (217) 693-4801
E-Mail: CERF@vmdb.org
www.vmdb.org

Orthopedic Foundation for Animals (OFA)
2300 E. Nifong Boulevard
Columbia, MO 65201-3806
Telephone: (573) 442-0418
Fax: (573) 875-5073
Email: ofa@offa.org
www.offa.org

US Food and Drug Administration Center for Veterinary Medicine (CVM)
7519 Standish Place
HFV-12
Rockville, MD 20855
Telephone: (240) 276-9300
Email: AskCVM@fda.hhs.gov
www.fda.gov/AnimalVeterinary/

Publications

Kennedy, Stacy. Animal Planet™ *Complete Guide to Puppy Care*. TFH Publications, Inc., 2000, 2012.

Leach, Laurie. *The Beginner's Guide to Dog Agility*. TFH Publications, Inc., 2006.

Libby, Tracy. *High-Energy Dogs*. TFH Publications, Inc., 2010.

Swager, Peggy. *Training the Hard-to-Train Dog*. TFH Publications, Inc., 2009.

Websites

Nylabone
www.nylabone.com

TFH Publications, Inc.
www.tfh.com

Index

Note: **Boldface** numbers indicate illustrations.

Photo Credits

Adya (Shutterstock.com): 244
AlikeYou (Shutterstock.com): 174
Andrei Rybachuk (Shutterstock.com): back cover
Andrey Eremin (Shutterstock.com): 74
Andriy Solovyov (Shutterstock.com): 137
AnetaPics (Shutterstock.com): 10, 63, 94, 142, 154, 222
Anna Hoychuk (Shutterstock.com): 14, 58, 70, 120, 224
Anneka (Shutterstock.com): 76
Annette Shaff (Shutterstock.com): 13, 100, 201
ARENA Creative (Shutterstock.com): 16, 26
ARTSILENSE (Shutterstock.com): 237
Barna Tanko (Shutterstock.com): 8, 60, 220
Basileus (Shutterstock.com): 15
Bauman (Shutterstock.com): 71
Becky Sheridan (Shutterstock.com): 136
Best dog photo (Shutterstock.com): 52
Bianca L (Shutterstock.com): 45
bluecrayola (Shutterstock.com): 217
BlueSkyImage (Shutterstock.com): 68
Calvin Chan (Shutterstock.com): 91
CBCK (Shutterstock.com): 41
Celeste Thomas: 89, 98 (sidebar left), 98 (sidebar center), 98 (sidebar right), 129 (sidebar left), 129 (sidebar center), 129 (sidebar right), 170, 175 (sidebar left), 175 (sidebar center), 175 (sidebar right), 178 (sidebar left), 178 (sidebar center), 178 (sidebar right), 184 (sidebar left), 184 (sidebar center), 184 (sidebar right), 187 (sidebar left), 187 (sidebar center), 190 (sidebar left), 190 (sidebar right), 195 (sidebar left), 195 (sidebar center), 195 (sidebar right), 205 (sidebar left), 205 (sidebar center), 205 (sidebar right), 209 (sidebar), 215 (sidebar)
Charles Brutlag (Shutterstock.com): 139
Chris Alcock (Shutterstock.com): 210
Christian Mueller (Shutterstock.com): 43, 135, 179
Claire McAdams (Shutterstock.com): 6
cynoclub (Shutterstock.com): 31, 204, 231
dexter_cz (Shutterstock.com): 59
Dieter Hawlan (Shutterstock.com): 75
dogboxstudio (Shutterstock.com): 27, 42, 130
Dora Zett (Shutterstock.com): 93, 96
Dorottya Mathe (Shutterstock.com): 5, 247
DragoNika (Shutterstock.com): 34

Duncan Andison (Shutterstock.com): 12, 66
Eldad Carin (Shutterstock.com): 208
Eric Isselee (Shutterstock.com): front cover, 11, 33, 79, 155, 173, 225, 227, 241, 242
Erik Lam (Shutterstock.com): 47
Ermolaev Alexander (Shutterstock.com): 1, 57, 86, 223, 233, 251
Gayane (Shutterstock.com): 144
gillmar (Shutterstock.com): 4
gorillaimages (Shutterstock.com): 128
gpointstudio (Shutterstock.com): 82
Halfpoint (Shutterstock.com): 150
Hannamariah (Shutterstock.com): 140
Harald Lueder (Shutterstock.com): 172
iko (Shutterstock.com): 29, 171
Igor Normann (Shutterstock.com): 198
Jagodka (Shutterstock.com): 35, 69, 83, 189, 228, 236
Jakkrit Orrasri (Shutterstock.com): 181
Jari Hindstroem (Shutterstock.com): 49
Javier Brosch (Shutterstock.com): 39
Joyce Marrero (Shutterstock.com): 17
KannaA (Shutterstock.com): page borders (paw-print pattern), Trainer Talk borders (paw-print pattern)
KAZLOVA IRYNA (Shutterstock.com): 18
KellyNelson (Shutterstock.com): 44
Kichigin (Shutterstock.com): 157
Kinga (Shutterstock.com): 80
Kuznetsov Alexey (Shutterstock.com): 81
Larisa Lofitskaya (Shutterstock.com): 77
Laurie Leach: 156, 161, 163, 168 (left), 168 (right), 187 (sidebar right), 197 (sidebar), 213 (sidebar)
l i g h t p o e t (Shutterstock.com): 48
Lionel Alvergnas (Shutterstock.com): 196
Lisa A (Shutterstock.com): 202
L. Nagy (Shutterstock.com): 185
Lostry7 (Shutterstock.com): 132
Lynn Watson (Shutterstock.com): 125
Makarova Viktoria (Shutterstock.com): 24
MANDY GODBEHEAR (Shutterstock.com): 7
margouillat photo (Shutterstock.com): 149
mariait (Shutterstock.com): 99
mdmmikle (Shutterstock.com): 122
mezzotint (Shutterstock.com): 30
mimagephotography (Shutterstock.com): 160
Monika Wisniewska (Shutterstock.com): 55
Monkey Business Images (Shutterstock.com): 72
Multiart (Shutterstock.com): 50
Nikolai Tsvetkov (Shutterstock.com): 191
Okssi (Shutterstock.com): 183

Orientgold (Shutterstock.com): 19
otsphoto (Shutterstock.com): 116, 134, 230
padu_foto (Shutterstock.com): 21, 67
Patryk Kosmider (Shutterstock.com): 192
Pavel Hlystov (Shutterstock.com): 232
PCHT (Shutterstock.com): 9
Phase4Studios (Shutterstock.com): 28
PhillipsC (Shutterstock.com): 40
picturepartners (Shutterstock.com): 193
Piotr Zajac (Shutterstock.com): 165
Poprotskiy Alexey (Shutterstock.com): 117
pryzmat (Shutterstock.com): 65, 88
Richard Peterson (Shutterstock.com): 46
Rita Kochmarjova (Shutterstock.com): 23, 51, 112, 226
Robynrg (Shutterstock.com): 106
Ross Stevenson (Shutterstock.com): 36
Sarah Lew (Shutterstock.com): 114
Scorpp (Shutterstock.com): 61, 101
Sergej Razvodovskij (Shutterstock.com): 199
Shutterstock.com: 214
S.I.A (Shutterstock.com): 73
Smit (Shutterstock.com): 127
Soloviova Liudmyla (Shutterstock.com): 37
Stocked House Studio (Shutterstock.com): 64
stocker1970 (Shutterstock.com): 32
Susan Schmitz (Shutterstock.com): 54
Svetlana Prikhnenko (Shutterstock.com): front cover (paw-print pattern), back cover (paw-print pattern), spine (paw-print pattern)
Tasha Thomson: 200 (sidebar), 217 (sidebar)
Toshe Ognjanov (Shutterstock.com): 84
TravnikovStudio (Shutterstock.com): 194
Vera Zinkova (Shutterstock.com): 78
Viktor1 (Shutterstock.com): 53
Viorel Sima (Shutterstock.com): 234
WilleeCole Photography (Shutterstock.com): 25, 62, 102, 108, 167, 176, 235, 248, 253
Zuzana Susterova (Shutterstock.com): 38
Zuzule (Shutterstock.com): 22, 218

All other photos courtesy of TFH and Nylabone archives.

ACKNOWLEDGMENTS

I want to extend a sincere thank you to the people who helped me complete this book. First, I am immensely grateful to Celeste Thomas, who offered her editing skills and thoughtful insights about teaching pups. I also want to thank C.J. Thomson, who critiqued each word from a novice trainer's perspective.

My appreciation also goes to Lauri Plummer, who shared her experiences about raising her pup Jade; Laurel Scarioni, who let me visit her training classes and include several of her training exercises; and Canine Companions puppy raisers, who served as models for many of the activities and photos.

ABOUT THE AUTHOR

Laurie Leach has had an eclectic dog training career. She has trained and raced sled dogs, competed in agility at the local and national level with multiple dogs, and taught classes for hundreds of future assistance dogs. Based on her experiences, Laurie came to believe that pups and dogs are both smarter and more emotional than you might expect. She set out to design a program for stimulating and stretching puppy minds and has shared this program for raising a gifted puppy with many clients. Now this program is available to you. Laurie hopes that once you get started, you will find it impossible to conceive of teaching your puppy less. Laurie lives in Windsor, California.

Nylabone®

Safe, Healthy Chewing
Since 1955

Nylabone® treats and dog chews are designed to meet the various chewing styles and strengths of every size and breed of dog.

Nylabone Products
P.O. Box 427, Neptune NJ 07754-0427 • Fax 732-988-5466
www.nylabone.com • info@nylabone.com
For more information contact your sales representative or contact us at sales@nylabone.com

CENTRAL
Garden & Pet